Church and Human Sexuality

Titles in this Series

Church and Human Sexuality

Arvind Theodore

2020

Church and Human Sexuality - jointly published by the Indian Society for Promoting Christian Knowledge (ISPCK), Post Box 1585, Kashmere Gate, Delhi-110006 and Council for World Mission, Singapore-338729.

ISBN: 978-93-88945-80-6

Kindle Edition: 978-93-88945-93-6

Cover Picture Credit : Immanuel Paul Vivekanandh K

Laser typeset by

ISPCK, Post Box 1585, 1654, Madarsa Road, Kashmere Gate, Delhi-110006 • *Tel:* 23866323

e-mail: ashish@ispck.org.in • ella@ispck.org.in
website: www.ispck.org.in

*This book was made possible through
the kind contribution of the Council for World Mission*

Dedication

I dedicate this book to my beloved parents, Prasanna Kumari Anandan and Dhanaraj Anandan, and my dear brother, Arun Samuel David. I am what I am because of their love and sacrifice.

Contents

Foreword

DISCERNMENT AND RADICAL ENGAGEMENT (DARE) is an initiative of the Council for World Mission (CWM) to enable faith communities to *clarify what it means to engage in* public witness to God's justice and peace in a corrupt and conflicted world.

> The mission of DARE is conceived as the coming together of (a) the *radical soul* of discernment and sense-making in theology and biblical criticism; (b) the yearnings for *signifying engagement* that rise out of the slums of modernism and the valleys of despair; and (c) the commitment to redemption songs that *inspire disturbance* at the hubs of power.

As part of the DARE initiative, each region of CWM is invited to prepare and share biblical and theological resources on current themes and issues being considered by CWM, drawing upon the experiences and resources from the region.

Interfaith Engagement, Ecumenism and Inclusive communities against dehumanising social categorisations are the themes for the book series undertaken by the South Asia region of CWM. The thrust is centred on Reimagining Church as Event: Perspectives from the Margins. It calls to the fore persons living in the margins and highlights their voice, their narratives and their passion for a rearrangement of life in communities, as we know it, and a commitment to rise to life and to break out from Babylon. These books are intended for the use of lay people, pastors and evangelists as well as for theological students and seminaries. The series offer stories and narratives, analyses, liturgical resources, biblical, theological and ethical reflections, and missional/praxis proposals.

Church is an event that happens at the margins of contemporary life. Church happens as an epiphanic event where the divine presence is manifested and experienced in the pathos, struggles, contestations and harmonies of everyday existence. Church happens in those spaces where we celebrate the presence of Jesus, the Christ, in the flourishing of life. Church happens when we are transformed by one another, and inspired and enabled to engage in the transformative politics of the reign of God. Church happens whenever and wherever spirit-filled communities reclaim their subversive moral agency and contest the logic and practices of domination and exclusion. Church happens when the community experiences the healing power of the wounded healer and join Jesus in this risk-taking mission, despite the wounds we bear. To reimagine Church requires courage and commitment to engage in the mission of nurturing and organising communities of resistance and healing. This book series is a humble attempt at exposing and encouraging this radical expression of Church.

I appreciate and thank all those who are associated with this series, the authors, the contributors, the publishers and the editors. I commend this book series in the hope and prayers that they will help the faith communities in South Asia, and beyond, to *discern God's presence in community and dare to engage* in ways that re-present the God of life in communities and in the public square, *Rising to Life: Living out the New Heaven and New Earth.*

Colin Cowan
General Secretary
Council for World Mission

Introduction

*Winnie Varghese**

If, as Arvind Theodore proposes, God loves diversity and justice, what would God's church look like? Theodore proposes a queer, sexual, and repentant community. As an Episcopal priest, I find this proposal convincing and compelling.

For the work we need to do among ourselves as Christians, this book is a wonderful resource to challenge the theological and cultural biases we bring to our reading of the Bible and our reading of one another. This text addresses the major arguments for homophobia and limitation of gender expression in the church, along with faithful scholarly and pastoral responses that define an inclusive, repentant way forward.

For Christians, because of political movements in the West, sexuality and gender have taken primacy of place in the landscape of our controversies. While race, caste, ecology, and class can also be cast as urgent social issues that call on the church for a gospel lens to be applied, sexuality and gender have taken priority in Christianity worldwide, often manipulated by those in power to maintain the status quo with a hint of scandal. I know I do not want scandal in my life. I would guess the same for you.

That status quo includes sexual abuse with impunity by those in power, and enforced repression or suppression of sexuality within the church, administered by believers on one another through codes of respectability or decency that often reflect cultural norms rather than a theological or ethical Christian position.

Arvind Theodore proposes a church that takes the doctrines of creation, incarnation, crucifixion, and resurrection seriously by acknowledging the centrality of human bodies and their desires to these primary doctrines of Christian theology.

I will admit that this vision of church seems a long way away to me, and yet, I cannot state with integrity that any part of what is proposed is not true to the witness of Jesus who finds himself vulnerable in his embodiment; chooses to be among outsiders; makes of himself a scandal; and closes the deal by appearing in a death-defying, previously unknown physical form. As Theodore argues, there probably is no institution more queer than the church, and nothing more homophobic.

I believe the illusion of respectability is among the curses of racism, brought to India in the colonial era and in some ways expressed in casteism. When the church becomes an instrument of power, a respectable institution that conveys respectability, an institution that should embody scandal becomes the carrier of power, mission and empire. For this, repentance is our proper posture; with humility we must acknowledge that LGBTQ+ people might never find our churches a safe or desirable place to be because of our community's attitudes, but we must also be clear that we are working as hard as we can to be inclusive and welcoming so that generations to come will not know the church as a place of oppression.

It is critical to think about gender and sex in the Indian context for the Indian theological project and for the sake of the Christian witness in India. Let us not forget that the world can see us. They can see our internal struggles with power: power over; power to silence; and shared power. The world can see our witness to inclusion. It was joked at the time of the review of Section 377 of the Indian Penal Code, that the diverse religious communities of India can rarely be brought together on any issue, but on homophobia, they all quickly agreed. We should be ashamed.

One of the many reasons this conversation is difficult is the shame we have been taught should apply to matters of sexuality. Professor Carter Heyward's work, which is cited in this text, places the creative power of God at the centre of sexuality but with the subtle shift from a focus on reproductive possibility as creative power to a body's pleasure as creative power.

It is important to think about power, coercion, and consent in this conversation, but it is also necessary to talk about the purpose of sexuality, and with the same critical lens we apply to colonial theories of peoples and land, look critically at the very problematic medieval European ideas of science and gender that undergird traditional theology on sexuality and marriage.

One inheritance of Christianity is a denial of the body. Paul writes that marriage is not a good in itself, but a way to avoid sexual transgression. Paul writes within the context of diverse gender and sexual expressions in what is now the Middle East and Europe, and he rejects them all as inferior to celibacy in anticipation of the return of Jesus and the end time. That is not the teaching of the Protestant churches today.

As Christians, we must note that the Bible holds within it a range of views on human sexuality that are not ours today. The stories of creation call the original human a being of the earth, an earth creature, and in one story, containing at least two genders and then split into two parts—the early patriarchs have multiple wives, notably foreign wives, and those families are fraught with stories of seduction, violation, rape, and sex workers. They are stories that tell us much about the human condition, but they cannot be read as prescriptive regarding gender or sexuality. Rather, they are multivalent and speak in multiple voices, at times arresting our sense of what is the permanent, historically held truth. In the Bible we read of multiple genders and intimacy between people of the same gender. When we get to the New Testament, we hear very little about sex and gender from Jesus, and not much from Paul either. This is apparent when we consider how much of Christian life is centred around the family. Neither Jesus nor Paul spend much time on it. They are more focused on the community of followers, disciples, and later the church. This leaves us with very little teaching about gender and sexuality in the Bible except, depending upon your translation, restrictions on participating in sexual acts of devotion in temples, and Paul's advice not to ever have sex, if you can avoid it.

This leaves Christians with the task of understanding family, sex and gender with the best scientific and philosophical resources of our time. How do sex and gender work in our bodies and minds? How is it theorised? What is the responsibility of one human being to another, to society overall? What are the purposes of the biological functions of our bodies? And, how do the ways we can use our bodies bear witness to God? What is our witness to be?

I find the proposals in this text self-critical, dialogical, and prayerful next steps to becoming a more faithful church following Jesus who made himself a scandal that the world might know God anew.

* **The Rev. Winnie Varghese** is a priest on the Strategic Clergy team at Trinity Church Wall Street, New York, USA. She is a blogger for Patheos; author of *Church Meets World*; editor of *What We Shall Become*; and author of numerous articles and chapters on social justice and the church.

Acknowledgement

This book could not have been written without the support of many. It roughly represents about seven years of reflection on the topic of sexuality, and is an outcome of seminars and academic writings, and conversations, dialogues and disagreements with professors, students, friends and family. I am indebted to the Council for World Mission for the opportunity to contribute to the Discernment and Radical Engagement (DARE) book series. My heartfelt thanks to the series editors George Zachariah and Sudipta Singh for their patience and trust. I specifically wish to thank George Zachariah, who was my professor at the United Theological College, Bengaluru, for mentoring and guiding me in my academic journey and in the process of writing this book. I am thankful to The Reverend Winnie Varghese and John Lalnuntluanga for contributing the Introduction and Afterword respectively. It would be remiss of me not to acknowledge the copy editor, Samuel Abraham, for his invaluable editorial corrections. My special and grateful thanks to Yajenlemla, Esther Parajuli, Immanuel Nehemiah and Samuel Ragland Paul who helped in different capacities by encouraging me, introducing me to new ideas and concepts, and in being conversation partners at various periods of time. Finally, with deep gratitude and admiration, I dedicate this book to my beloved parents, Prasanna Kumari Anandan and Dhanaraj Anandan, and my dear brother, Arun Samuel David. I am what I am because of their love and sacrifice.

Prologue

The prevailing dominant understanding of sexuality is constructed and construed within a hetero-patriarchal context, resulting in sex-negativity, subordination and abuse of persons, and the invalidation of non-normative sexual expressions and bodily desires. In light of this sexual crisis, and in recognition of the challenges the Indian Church and faith communities are confronted with, this book is a theo-ethical inquiry about sexuality. In the continued effort to address the moral perplexities people are faced with, this book is just one of the many attempts in recent years in carrying on the prophetic work of confronting the historical layers of scriptural and cultural meanings that have proven to be ruinous to peoples and communities, and in excavating new meanings and insights that have the potential to contribute to healing, freedom and sexual justice.

I would not be surprised if one of the first questions that came to your mind upon seeing the book were, "Why is a heterosexual person writing about sexuality and the LGBTQ+ community?" (assuming that you already know me and my sexual orientation). It is a legitimate question and you are perfectly entitled to it. The significance of this question lies in the politics of representation. As objectivity, says Miguel De La Torre, is a

Eurocentric demand, the book resists the idea that objectivity is the way to go.[1] This means the book is a *subjective* analysis and interpretation of human sexuality, and the *subjectivity* of the content is coloured by my gender and sexual orientation. My identity as a cisgender heterosexual male, without a shadow of doubt, influences my thinking about sexuality and, in turn, the content of the book.

I must make this clear: the book is not written for the LGBTQ+ community as they do not need another heterosexual person telling them what to do. It is written for people like myself to come to terms with the hard yet emancipatory truth that our liberation is inextricably bound to theirs. During the many months of putting words to pages, I have learnt to embrace my identity and love my body with all its fascinations and limitations. In the process, I have realised that many have been prevented from loving themselves, their bodies and desires shamed. Undertaking this project has helped me understand how my compliance with systems of oppression impedes human flourishing. The book, in many ways, is a process of auditing myself and coming to terms with my own sexuality and the reality of being located in a position of power as a heterosexual and as a male. In acknowledging the privileged access to connections, spaces and knowledge my identity grants me, the ethical challenge is to exercise those privileges (not all, for many need to be expunged) towards radical transformation. Therefore, recognising and challenging my sense of entitlement and substituting oppressive beliefs and morals for liberative ones that contribute to the well-being of all becomes an ethical task. After all, the ethical is political.

Added to the subjectivity is my identity as a Dalit. Joshua Samuel, in his recent essay "Towards a Queer Dalit Theology:

Dialogue and Solidarity Among the Margins," urges Dalit Theology, and by extension Dalits, to take seriously the concerns of the LGBTQ+ community.[2] While differences and specificities in experiences of oppression and marginalisation exist and must be respected, the similarities in being considered an outcast and an abomination to/by the dominant culture compels me to confront (sexual) injustices, particularly in relation to those branded as "weak," "immoral," and "pervert." Therefore, as a Dalit I have absolutely no excuse for not standing up against sexism and heterosexism just the way I do to casteism. No oppressed community can stand and work for its liberation in isolation; it needs the support of other communities through acts of solidarity. Sundar John Boopalan puts it rather candidly when he says, "Solidarity is no solidarity if it is only for an imagined 'our own.'"[3]

It might occur to you at some point of reading that I am being rather heavily critical of the Indian Church. But is it not true that the Indian Church is deeply sexist and heterosexist? Is it not true that the Indian Church prefers to stay quiet on issues of sexual violence? Having been part of different churches for varied periods of time, I can certainly testify to it, in varying degrees of course. While my Christian identity adds another layer to the subjectivity of the content as I do not make claims on other religious traditions, I believe calling out the injustices perpetuated by the Church is part of my Christian calling, a crucial part of Christian discipleship. Naming the Church's sins is unquestionably a holy act. As a person rooted in the Christian faith, I am bound to be responsible and just in my relationships and social interactions, and to be a voice of dissent, calling those in ecclesial authority to be accountable to those at the margins. I am critical of the Church because I love the Church.

Ashley Tellis impels us to be "… constantly vigilant of the axis of our own formation and the limits they impose on how we experience the world."[4] I cannot tell you how pivotal this is given the ongoing debates on allyship. An ally is one who is not part of the LGBTQ+ community but stands in solidarity with them. While some include "ally" in their definition of queer, there are those who question its inclusion within the larger queer community simply because ally is not an identity. An ally still has the privileges and rights that queer people do not. An exasperated Dianna Anderson writes, "The centering of your own privilege becomes so important that you think a movement cannot possibly survive without your essential leadership and ally-behavior."[5] Anderson is basically putting heterosexuals in their place. The catalysts for transformation are not the allies, like myself or the Church, but queers themselves. The opinions and suggestions of an ally are never more valid than the ones who are part of the community.

The right to see me as an ally rests with the LGBTQ+ community. I cannot insist that I am, and quite frankly I should not. Doing so eliminates their agency and justifies the arrogance of paternalism. My sexual orientation quite evidently precludes me from speaking on their behalf. No heterosexual voice can be a legitimate substitute for a queer voice. As an ally, I can only lend my support in solidarity; I cannot script alternative paths to liberation. Any attempt to do the latter is to ignore the wisdom of their bodies. Yet, when Christian ministers and self-proclaimed apostles and prophets categorically state that the reason for pandemics and natural disasters is homosexuality and abortion, to remain silent is a grave sin. Given the moral bankruptcy of the Church and those beyond its borders, participating in the collective struggle for liberation is my bounden duty. Failure to act ends up contributing to the tyranny of the dominant.

Commenting on the politics of representation within the Indian film industry, Dalit film director and producer Pa. Ranjith says, "There is nothing more violent than occupying someone else's space."[6] This is true with just about any oppressed community. Voices from the community should never be substituted for any other. Likewise, Marvin Ellison rightly observes, "… gay people are talked about and spoken to, but we are not listened to, learnt from, or granted our moral authority as shapers of religious and moral traditions."[7] This book, in incorporating queer voices, presses the Church to stop speaking and listen to the ones who have the power to liberate us from apathy and self-centredness. It cautions against disabling queer agency through imprudent activism. It is absolutely critical that you and I learn to listen, listen not to respond but to learn. Philip Peacock reminds us that queer voices need to be heard and the allies may have to provide that space.[8] The act of providing space is not a manifestation of heterosexual (male) privilege but rather an outcome of the decentring of privilege.

Even as the book makes reference to the LGBTQ+ community projecting them as subjects of their own liberation, it is primarily a reminder that we are all sexual beings. Engaging with sexuality is imperative for everyone as it allows for a better and healthier understanding of our bodies and refines and facilitates our commitment toward sexual justice. Sexuality is perhaps the least talked about topic in the Church and in our homes. As cliché as it sounds, it is nevertheless true. It is time, if it were not already, to come to a place where we can embrace our bodies and sexualities and talk freely about it without having to feel embarrassed or ashamed. Importantly, we ought to let others talk about it *freely*.

Susanne Scholz begins one of her essays with a catchy theological statement: "God loves diversity and justice."[9] This is undoubtedly true even as it affirms the book's theological position. So, I invite you to read with an open mind, recognise the diversity around you, and commit your minds, hearts, and bodies to the prophetic work of sexual justice.

Endnotes

[1] I use the term Eurocentrism to refer to a worldview that privileges the dominant, and not as a geographically determined term.

[2] Consider reading, Joshua Samuel, "Towards a Queer Dalit Theology: Dialogue and Solidarity Among the Margins," *Bangalore Theological Forum*, vol. LI, No.2 (2019): 142-167.

[3] John Boopalan, Instagram post, August 9, 2019.

[4] Ashley Tellis, "Disrupting the Dinner Table: Re-thinking the 'Queer Movement' in Contemporary India," in *Jindal Global Law Review*, 4:1 (August 2012): 150,

http://www.academia.edu/4066880/Disrupting_the_Dinner_Table_Rethinking_the_Queer_Movement_in_Contemporary_India (accessed June 10, 2020).

[5] Dianna E. Anderson, "I'm Not Your Ally: The Problem of Ally-As-Identity,

http://diannaeanderson.net/blog/2013/10/im-not-your-ally-the-problem-of-ally-as-identity (accessed June 14, 2020).

[6] Udhav Naig, "From 'Attakathi' to 'Kabali' to 'Pariyerum Perumal': How this decade changed Caste representation in Kollywood, *The Hindu*,

https://www.thehindu.com/entertainment/movies/from-attakathi-and-kabali-to-pariyerum-perumal-how-this-decade-changed-caste-representation-in-kollywood/article30432918.ece (accessed June 22, 2020).

[7] Marvin M. Ellison, "What God Hath Joined: Notes on Same-Sex Marriage and Justice Making," in *Union Seminary Quarterly Review*, 53:3-4 (1999): 112. Cited in, George Zachariah, "Introduction," in *Disruptive Faith, Inclusive Communities: Church and Homophobia*, eds. George Zachariah and Vincent Rajkumar (Bangalore/Delhi: CISRS/ISPCK, 2015), xxiii.

[8] E-mail message from the National Council of Churches in India, March 19, 2017.

[9] Susanne Scholz (ed.), "Introduction: From Progressive Theological Discourse to Changing the World," in *God Loves Diversity and Justice: Progressive Scholars Speak about Faith, Politics, and the World* (New York/ Toronto: Lexington Books, 2013), 1.

1

Problematising Sexuality

India is a country with multiple peoples, cultures, languages and faiths, and also a country deeply rooted in multiple structures of oppressions such as casteism, patriarchy, capitalism, racism, colourism, xenophobia and heterosexism. In recent decades, discourses on sexuality in India have come to the fore and it has been approached with a conglomerate of emotions of fear, aversion, passion, anxiety and *eros*. Due to the lack of affirmations regarding sexuality by the Church, the task of addressing the very intricate being of a person has been neglected, resulting in an ignorant, distorted and negative view of sexuality.[1] Most people are uncomfortable in talking about sexuality as it has often been associated with sin, and it is precisely due to this "sexuality-sin" nexus that violence and injustice have been the outcome. Indubitably, it leaves many questioning, suppressing and hiding the knowledge of their own sexuality, fearing rejection, guilt and shame. At a time when peoples' right to desire is pillaged it is imperative for faith communities to respond, and respond with a sense of responsibility and love.

Sex and Gender

The mistake one often tends to make is in using sex and gender synonymously. This is wrong. Sex and gender are distinguishable. Sex refers to the biological male and female, while gender refers to the social constructions attached to the male and female categories. Categorisation of sex is based on biological differences related to hormonal and reproductive differences. One must be aware that intersex is another assigned sex like male or female, and intersexed persons need not have ambiguous genitalia (intersexed persons are not transgenders as intersex is a sex category and transgender is a gender category).[2]

Gender, on the other hand, implies meanings that society, cultures and individuals give to male and female categories.[3] It is a social construct. Social, parental, peer and media influences contribute to gender development, affirming it as an experienced, instructed and learnt activity.[4] It is important to note that one's sex does not determine one's gender, and gender is neither fixed nor given. While there are three categories of sex (male, female and intersex), Gopi Shankar notes that there are over fifty-eight categories of gender.[5] So one could say that sex is biological (and given) while gender is socially constructed. However, philosopher and gender theorist Judith Butler understands sex to be a social construct as well.[6]

What is Queer?

Over the decades the term queer has gained popularity and has been used as a prefix to methodologies, theologies, ethics, theories and scientific studies. Often interpreted as "strange," "odd," "peculiar," "to spoil," etc., the term was hurled as an insult at anyone who did not fit in. Finding the term offensive, the LGBTQ+ community subverted and redefined it, using it as a sign of pride, representing their desires and interests.[7] Kath Browne and Catherine J. Nash note that the term queer, to be faithful to its ontological nature, means to remain unclear, fluid and multiple. It occupies a non-normative position in being unstable and undefinable.[8] So to define the term is to demarcate its functionality, which is problematic. The term, in symbolising ambiguity, dispels any fixed, permanent and categorical definitions. As much as this is right and true, I find it essential to state how the term is being used in this book to provide clarity to readers, while reminding myself and the readers that the term embodies vast usages and possibilities of usages.

Patrick S. Cheng, an Asian theologian, provides three different ways the term queer can be used: Queer as an Umbrella term, Queer as Transgressive Action, and Queer as Erasing Boundaries.[9] By using queer as an umbrella term, he implies that it refers collectively to lesbian, gay, bisexual, transgender, intersex, questioning, and all those individuals who do not identify with normative constructions of sexual and gender identities.[10] The second usage seeks to reclaim the word and embrace it with pride as it stands in opposition to all norms that are considered normative. And the third usage, seeks to challenge, disrupt, and erase fixed categories such as female/male or homosexual/heterosexual. Here, sexual and gender categories are deconstructed to affirm sexual and gender fluidity. Therefore, a queer, if personified, is a person who stands in opposition to heterosexuals, affirming one's own identity by rejecting fixed given normative categories and the dominant hetero-patriarchal culture. If used as a methodological approach, it questions the existence of and disembowels social normative claims, hierarchies, and power relations.

Human Sexuality

One of the biggest misconceptions people have while discussing human sexuality is in narrowing it down to LGBTQ+ communities. This is fallacious. Any discourse on sexuality must concern the sexuality of every individual.[11] As noted in the preface, the book ultimately is a reminder that all of us are sexual beings. Yet, the problem is in not considering all sexual beings right and equal. If people are categorised into normal and abnormal, sacred and profane, honourable and pervert, the categorisations and the basis for such categorisations need to be tackled and uprooted. For this reason, I must concede that there would be sections where a conscious reference would be made to LGBTQ+ communities. In doing so, I clarify that there is no academic fascination with their sexualities. I make reference to them to point to the myriad ways we have been conditioned with a heteronormative understanding of sexuality, resulting in controlling and regulating of non-normative sexualities, bodies and desires. This, I believe, needs to be confronted.

Theodore Jennings notes that the word sexuality is theologically, socially and culturally interpreted as a site for struggle against sin.[12] Anything to do with sexuality is considered profane, obscene and indecent. This has caused many to moralise sexuality rather than celebrate it. One must, however, remember that humans are essentially sexual creatures, and so sexuality is central to human life, intrinsically part of one's personality. But what is sexuality? What does it include? Sexuality can be understood as a personal orientation of desire that manifests in diverse forms permeating and affecting one's thoughts, feelings and actions. In plain terms, it can mean the capacity to have erotic experiences, to love, and to be sexually attracted to another person. For James Nelson, sexuality includes one's attitude towards one's body and those of others as it causes us to reach out to others and embrace them both physically and spiritually.[13] It is, "our total, embodied, sensuous connection to all things," as Beverly Harrison would put it.[14]

Moving further, I wish to lay before you the argument that sexuality is both given and not given. By saying it is given, I intend to state that sexuality is intrinsic to us. This means we cannot undo the dispositions with which we are born. By saying it is not given, I state that it could be a choice that persons consciously make for themselves.[15] While its foundations are biological, it develops over a period of time within a human environment. And since human environments never cease to change, sexuality should be seen as having a fluid nature and not being confined to and interpreted within fixed, given and non-negotiable categories. If sexuality is limited to its biological frontiers alone, the enormous potency of the symbolic meanings it bears is negated. Since the "nature vs. nurture" thesis is open to debate, I leave it to you to explore.

The Early Church's Understanding of Sexuality

If sexuality needs to be seen as a justice issue, we must first know what contributes to sexual injustice. For that we begin with the understanding of sexuality that has been perpetuated by the Church. The Early Church Fathers' apprehension and perception of sexuality has contributed much to our present and problematic understandings of sexuality. Their profound distaste for sexuality still adds to the further oppression of sexual and gender minorities.

It can be said that the ancestors of our faith understood sexuality very differently from the way it is understood today. Or, at least, the way it *should* be understood today. For them, sexuality could not be intertwined with love, and since sex and sexuality was equated to sin and lust, celibacy was adulated. Clement of Rome, in his defence of marriage using stoic arguments, eliminated bodily love and sexual desire.[16] Augustine of Hippo went so far as to state that sexual intercourse between Adam and Eve could have taken place without the element of sexual desire as desire to him was intrinsically sinful.[17] Thomas Aquinas' understanding of sexuality could be inferred from his idea of marriage, which he saw as being monogamous and heterosexual, having procreation as its ultimate end.[18]

Eric Fuchs points out that many Eastern theologians, influenced by Origen, held the abysmal view that marriage and sexuality were consequences of the original sin.[19] Martin Luther and John Calvin, appearing several centuries later, affirmed human sexuality as part of God's divine plan and therefore was good, but being informed by Augustine's pessimistic view of fallen human nature and its distorted sex drive, believed that sexuality was sullied by lust. So, Luther and Calvin saw marriage as a remedy for sexual passion.[20] The historian Stephen Garton remarks that it was ingrained in people that one could attain salvation only by the renunciation of one's sexual desire and the devaluation of one's sexuality.[21] As sexual renunciation was seen as the emblem of human freedom, the body was admired in its virgin state and despised in its sexually active state. While one could easily brush aside this understanding of sexuality as crude and ancient, it continues to infiltrate our minds and influence our patterns of social interaction today. Is the Church's understanding of sexuality today then different to that of the old? Not really.

Sexuality as a Justice Issue

The topic of sexuality, within Indian Christian communities, is still a taboo. Even if one terms this statement as naïve or clichéd, it does not change the fact that sexuality is hardly, if ever, talked about. The Church's and Christians' hesitation to address issues such as marital rape, child abuse and masturbation is a testament to the sexuality-sin nexus that underlies and pervades much of our understanding of human sexuality. As Aruna Gnanadason asserts, "The churches rarely affirm the beauty of the female and male human body and the God-given gift of pleasure that it offers."[22] Truly, sex has been made *unimportant*.[23]

Marvin Ellison views sexuality as a crisis within a crisis. He writes: "The crisis of sexuality is revealed, in part, by persistently distorted, highly negative attitudes about sex, the human body, women, and other marginalized people."[24] The eroticising of dominant-subordinate social relations and the distortion of love only seem to compound this crisis. Feelings of control and violence supersede mutual erotic expressions.[25] This, Ellison regards, grants "social privilege to some at the disadvantage of others."[26] In the same vein, Nelson states how self-control, one of the "fruits of the Spirit," has easily slipped into "bodily mortification—the death of the flesh."[27] Since our understanding of sexuality and sexual mores are determined by legalism and authoritarianism, we idolise chastity, asceticism, celibacy and libidinal sexual repression.[28]

The low valuation of our bodies and our sexualities is also a cause for concern. We are taught and repeatedly warned to suppress our bodily passions and desires. This has drastically contributed to body-negativity. Consider women's sexuality: the fact that shame, guilt and uncleanliness are still attached to the bodily functions of menstruation and childbirth is appalling. Abortion is blindly termed as a sin without looking at the context and concern of the girls and women involved. Same-sex relationship is perceived as demonic and a perversion of sexuality because the Bible forbids same-sex *acts*.[29] People who have been infected with HIV/AIDS have been ostracised and accused of profanity. Because we have been misinformed and ill informed, and worse accepted them as the ultimate truth, we have directly and indirectly contributed to sexual injustice. Since these untruths have furthered oppression against women and LGBTQ+ communities, sexuality demands to be perceived as a justice issue. The ethical task before us is to challenge the crisis-contributing factors and question those norms that dehumanise persons.

When we speak of sexuality in terms of justice, we should be aware of categories such as power inequalities, social privilege and exploitation.[30] Harrison, in her analysis, mentions two problems with sexuality: sexuality being entangled in old dualisms, and in "distorted patterns of power-in-relations."[31] This is indicative of the power-powerless dynamic that characterises all sexual relations. Women's sexuality and desires are undermined, if not negated, and men's sexuality and desires are idealised and venerated. Think for a moment: Is not sexual activity considered complete only after the male has ejaculated? Women become nothing more than mere objects of pleasure. Therefore, the dominant understanding of sexuality needs to be critiqued and subverted in order to liberate human bodies from the clutches of power, control, ownership, manipulation and coercion. One can witness the flourishing of human personhood only when dominance and exploitation are replaced by mutuality and justice.

Another important point to help perceive sexuality as a justice issue is to understand sexuality as a structural problem. Carter Heyward calls structure a "pattern of relational transactions that gives a society its particular shape."[32] The meanings of sexuality take shape within the social and political contexts and conflicts of power, which in turn determine how society defines sexuality. Ellison mentions two approaches to understand sexuality: sexual essentialism and sexual constructivism. Sexual essentialism sees sexuality as non-negotiable, while sexual constructivism sees sexuality as a social construct within society and history.[33] The latter goes beyond biological definitions to assume sociocultural definitions. Because sexuality operates within these societal and cultural arrangements of power and powerlessness, it forms a pattern of relational transactions occurring between people in a way that accentuates and validates heteronormativity. When sexuality operates in this manner it elevates and validates only certain patterns of social relations, invalidating the rest. The validation and invalidation of social relations are then promulgated by sociocultural, political and religious institutions. These institutions, forming part of a larger structural arrangement, breed sexual injustice and social control. It is in and through these modes of operation that sexuality becomes a structural problem.

One of the foundational principles in Christian ethics is justice, and to deal with sexuality as a justice issue is to move from making "just love" to making "love just." Margaret Farley states that people's understanding of sexuality is submerged in the economy of defilement, sin, and guilt.[34] Due to this the principle of justice has not been advanced in love and sex. Looking at love and sex from the lens of justice allows one, Ellison contends, to address issues of power, question hierarchies, ensure fair distribution of material and intangible goods, challenge sex-negativity, and honour the goodness of the body.[35] It further allows one to affirm diversity in voices, identities, practices and experiences, and grants a certain privilege to the sexualities, perspectives and experiences of all people.[36] (Reminded of the statement "God loves diversity and justice?")

The Church must do away with an ethic of a former age and practice a new ethic that espouses freedom, friendship, intimacy, and love. Only then would themes such as the moral nature of sexual acts, subordination of women and effeminate men, procreation and same-sex love become more perceptible and discernible.[37] When this becomes obvious to the tabooed 'naked eye and mind,' ideas and perceptions regarding sexuality will begin to reorient and remodel. Our understanding of sexuality has certainly been marked by patches of sin and shame, contributing to sexual injustice. Yet, if sexuality is indispensable to humanity, we must fight the structures that perpetuate violations against human bodies.

Endnotes

[1] My usage of the word "Church" is in reference to the collective Indian Church. I use it as a catchall term while recognising and respecting the diversity and difference each church and faith community has to offer. Having been part of different churches, spanning across denominations and time periods, and not once having heard the church talk or address issues about sexuality, I find it safe to state that the Indian Church, by and large, holds a rather negative, if not ambiguous, view of sex. At any rate, one cannot deny the hetero-patriarchal influence behind the Church's understanding of sexuality.

[2] Gopi Shankar, "Definitions—Understanding Gender, Sex and Sexuality," in *A Theological Reader on Human Sexuality and Gender Diversities: Envisioning Inclusivity,* eds. Roger Gaikward and Thomas Ninan (Delhi/Nagpur: ISPCK/ NCCI, 2017), xx-xxi.

[3] Alice H. Eagly, "The Science and Politics of Comparing Women and Men: A Reconstruction," in *SAGE Handbook of Gender and Psychology*, eds. Michelle K. Ryan and Nyla R. Branscombe (London: SAGE Publications Limited, 2014), 21-22.

[4] Kay Bussey, "Gender Development," in *SAGE Handbook of Gender and Psychology*, eds. Michelle K. Ryan and Nyla R. Branscombe (London: SAGE Publications Limited, 2014), 83-91.

[5] "History of Gender Minorities in India – Gopi Shankar M," *Center for Indic Studies*, September 15, 2018, video, 7:20, https://www.youtube.com/watch?v=c7lYSwEaXzA&t=1188s (accessed June 11, 2020)

[6] For more information consider reading *Undoing Gender* and *Gender Trouble* by Judith Butler.

[7] Gerard Loughlin, "Introduction: End of Sex," in *Queer Theology: Rethinking the Western Body,* ed. Gerard Loughlin (Massachusetts: Blackwell Publishing, 2007), 7-8.

[8] Kath Browne and Catherine J. Nash (eds.), "Queer Methods and Methodologies: An Introduction," in *Queer Methods and Methodologies: Intersecting Queer Theories and Social Science Research* (London: Routledge, 2016), 7-8.

[9] Patrick S. Cheng, *An Introduction to Queer Theology: Radical Love* (New York: Seabury Books, 2011), 5-8.

[10] The representation of all sexual minorities under the term queer is not without flaws. As Theodore Jennings points out, the term queer can easily become a catchall that can negate the specificity and the tradition, practices, experience, and history of oppression of diverse sexualities, ignoring the heterogeneity within. See, Theodore W. Jennings, Jr., *An Ethic of Queer Sex: Principles and Improvisations* (Chicago: Exploration Press, 2013), 14. This is particularly true in the Indian context where the concerns and interests of lesbians and gays are privileged while those of transpersons, who predominantly are from socially excluded communities, are dismissed. With regard to my use of the term, I will, for the purpose of this book, employ the shorthand LGBTQ+, where "+" acknowledges the presence of other identities. One could certainly make a case that the "+" invisibilises other identities and leaves them underrepresented. This I cannot deny.

[11] This particular concern emerged from a member of the queer community during a NCCI (National Council of Churches in India) Seminar held at Bengaluru in April, 2016.

[12] Theodore W. Jennings, Jr., *An Ethic of Queer Sex: Principles and Improvisations* (Chicago: Exploration Press, 2013), 28.

[13] James B. Nelson, *Embodiment: An Approach to Sexuality and Christian Theology* (Minneapolis: Augsburg Publishing House, 1978), 17.

[14] Beverly Wildung Harrison, *Justice in the Making: Feminist Social Ethics* (Louisville: Westminster John Knox Press, 2004), 58.

[15] While homosexuality is not a choice, as many lesbians and gays express, homosexuality is also understood as a choice that individuals make for themselves. The moment sexuality is reduced to its biological governess, the right of individuals to make conscious choices is alienated. One's sexuality

should be one's freely chosen way of expressing one's humanness with any person that the individual wishes to do so without being biologically governed or necessitated. See, Rosemary Radford Ruether, "Homophobia, Heterosexism, and Pastoral Practice," in *Sexuality and the Sacred. Sources for Theological Reflection*, eds. James B. Nelson and Sandra P. Longfellow (Kentucky: John Knox Press, 1994), 396.

[16] Eric Fuchs, *Sexual Desire and Love: Origins and History of the Christian Ethic of Sexuality and Marriage*, trans. Marsha Daigle (New York: The Seabury Press, 1983), 92.

[17] Lisa Sowle Cahill, *Between the Sexes: Foundations for a Christian Ethics of Sexuality* (New York: Paulist Press, 1985), 2.

[18] Lisa Sowle Cahill, *Between the Sexes: Foundations for a Christian Ethics of Sexuality*, 106. Aquinas' understanding of sexuality was coloured by his moral theory called the Natural Law. To him, natural law was a body of principles written on the hearts of humans revealing a moral order that can be discovered only by reason. Natural law was God's plan for all and to violate it was to violate God. It was an attempt to arrive at universal morality. See, D. J. O'Connor. *Aquinas and Natural Law* (London: Macmillan & Co Ltd., 1967), 57-64. What does natural law have to do with his understanding of sexuality? For Aquinas procreation is the *telos* of sexual activity. Any spillage of semen is unnatural and sinful if it is not ejaculated into the genitalia of the opposite sex since semen is seen as the career of life. Any action that impedes or distorts the conjugal nature of the sexual act is wrong and immoral. Same-sex partners cannot procreate and are thus branded as "perverts." Since all sexual acts other than the penile-vaginal penetrative sex is non-generative, i.e., non-procreative, it violates the natural law.

[19] Eric Fuchs, *Sexual Desire and Love: Origins and History of the Christian Ethic of Sexuality and Marriage*, 98. Original Sin is an Augustinian doctrine that regards sin as inherent to humans as all are born sinful. The sin of Adam is passed on to generations through sexual intercourse. Romans 5:12 serves as the biblical justification for the doctrine. While Augustine says the original sin was disobedience, Ambrose and Jerome consider sex as the original sin. The doctrine contributes to the low valuation of sex and body.

[20] Margaret A. Farley, *Just Love: A Framework for Christian Sexual Ethics* (New York: Continuum International Publishing Group, 2006), 46.

[21] Stephen Garton, *Histories of Sexuality: Antiquity to Sexual Revolution* (London: Equinox Publishing Ltd, 2006), 49.

[22] Aruna Gnanadason, "Church and Sexual Morality," in *A Theological Reader on Human Sexuality and Gender Diversities: Envisioning Inclusivity,*

eds. Roger Gaikward and Thomas Ninan (Delhi/Nagpur: ISPCK/NCCI, 2017), 130.

[23] James B. Nelson, *Embodiment: An Approach to Sexuality and Christian Theology* (Minneapolis: Augsburg Publishing House, 1978), 71.

[24] Marvin M. Ellison, *Erotic Justice: A Liberating Ethic of Sexuality* (Kentucky: Westminster John Knox Press, 1996), 16.

[25] Beverly Wildung Harrison, *Making the Connections: Essays in Feminist Social Ethics,* ed. Carol S. Robb (Massachusetts: Beacon Press Books, 1985), 148.

[26] Marvin M. Ellison, *Making Love Just: Sexual Ethics for Perplexing Times* (Minneapolis: Fortress Press, 2012), 13.

[27] James B. Nelson, *Embodiment: An Approach to Sexuality and Christian Theology,* 71.

[28] Somen Das, *Christian Ethics and Indian Ethos* (New Delhi: ISPCK, 1994), 13.

[29] The Bible addresses same-sex acts and not same-sex identities. The difference is important. Since the term "homosexuality" is a late 19th century coinage, the authors of the Bible would have had no idea of this distinction. Today's understanding of sexuality is undoubtedly advanced than that of the biblical era.

[30] Marvin M. Ellison, *Making Love Just: Sexual Ethics for Perplexing Times,* 12.

[31] Beverly Wildung Harrison, *Justice in the Making: Feminist Social Ethics* (Louisville: Westminster John Knox Press, 2004), 60.

[32] Carter Heyward, *Touching Our Strength: The Erotic as Power and the Love of* God (San Francisco: Harper & Row, 1989), 50. Cited in, Marvin M. Ellison, *Erotic Justice: A Liberation Ethic of Sexuality* (Kentucky: Westminster John Knox Press, 1996), 32.

[33] Marvin M. Ellison, *Erotic Justice,* 33-34.

[34] She borrows these three symbols from Paul Ricoeur, who represents the stages of the experience of moral evil. For him, defilement resists reflection due to the fear of breaking taboos. Sin, for him, is the rupture of mutual relationships. And finally, guilt is the subjective awareness of sin within oneself. See, Paul Ricoeur, *Symbolism of Evil,* trans. Emerson Buchanan (New York: Harper & Row, 1967). Cited in, Margaret A. Farley, *Just Love: A Framework for Christian Sexual Ethics,* (London: Continuum International Publishing Group, 2006), 175-176.

[35] Marvin M. Ellison, *Making Love Just: Sexual Ethics for Perplexing Times,* 6 and 9.

[36] Theodore W. Jennings, Jr., *An Ethic of Queer Sex: Principles and Improvisations*, 193.

[37] Lisa Sowle Cahill, "Sexuality and Christian Ethics: How to Proceed," in *Sexuality and the Sacred: Sources for Theological Reflection*, eds. James B. Nelson and Sandra P. Longfellow (Kentucky: Westminster/John Knox Press, 1994), 25.

2

Sexuality and the Bible

The Church believes that morality is *revealed* in the Bible. In viewing the Bible and a long history of tradition as primary foundations for its sexual ethic, the Church makes it difficult to perceive sexuality in terms of love and affection.[1] The concept of "revealed morality" creates a form of moral discipline that grants ecclesial authorities the power to control the sexual desires and preferences of people. In order to have a renewed understanding of sexuality the idea of revealed morality needs to be done away with, and for it to be undone we must regard morality in the Bible as a product of its time.

Generally the Bible has been read in ways that show a profound distaste for sexuality, or, as some might note, its claims are rather ambiguous. The Garden of Eden narrative traditionally seen as an account of sexual sin, the Levitical laws used to demonise lesbians and gays, and texts in the New Testament used to view the *flesh* as carnal are some of the ways in which the Bible has been mis/used to distort sexuality.[2] God, in the Garden of Eden, created humans with the capacity to engage in sexual activity and declared it *good*

(Gen. 1:31). It was so good that God commanded humans to "be fruitful and multiply" (Gen 1:28).[3] However, this saying has come to mean that sex is only for procreation, thereby destabilising persons who cannot and do not want to conceive. Though sex is the source of future generations, it should not be confined to fulfilling the procreative purpose alone. This would be limiting the meaning, joy, and purpose of sexual activity.

While the Bible does contain some negative references to sexuality, J. Harold Ellens suggests that there is a positive contribution concerning sexuality as it views sex as integral to human relationships. Sexuality in the Bible, he argues, is about close connectedness, communion, and intimate mutuality between human persons.[4] This is suggestive that within the larger context of personhood and community, sexual intimacy in the Bible is viewed as being good. In order to take this discussion further, let us see what the First and Second Testaments have to say about sexuality.

Sexuality in the First Testament
The First Testament (commonly known as the Old Testament) contains materials that put sufficient boundaries on sexuality and sexual behaviour. It contains a plurality of customs, laws and insights related to sexuality. Nakedness was considered shameful and abhorrent, and random exposure of sexual organs was a taboo. Sexual purity laws were so stringent that sexual uncleanliness was understood as polluting the body and the land.[5] The First Testament's attitude towards sexuality was deeply influenced by patriarchal forms of sex, marriage and family, and due to the influence of the prophets,

the cultic notions of purity came to become profound moral concepts guiding the lives of people.[6]

That said, probably the most affirmative reference about sexuality in the First Testament is Genesis 1:22-27 implying God *is* sexual. There is something very essential to the very nature of God that is ultimately reflected in human nature.[7] Sex is God's thing! Human beings are created in the sexual nature of God. David Carr affirms God as an erotic Being as God created an erotic male and an erotic female.[8] In the creation story, there is no evidence of contempt for sexuality. Rather, it is that aspect of human life that must not be despised as evil for if it is done so, we miss out on the magnificence of experiencing and celebrating this divine gift. Furthermore, the very presence of the book of Songs of Songs shows that sexuality is both divine and divinely worldly in nature. Here, the poetic form employed, where lovers describe each other's bodies using images from nature and architecture, is known as *wasf* in Arabic. The portrayal of sexuality in this book is rich and imaginative even as it offers a glimpse of a return to Eden where humanity was naked and without shame, celebrating all creation, living in God's presence.[9] Finally, in speaking of the union between God and Israel, one cannot miss the use of erotic imagery. These First Testament references offer a more affirmative view of sexuality.

Sexuality in the Second Testament

The understanding and theology of sexuality in the Second Testament is historically conditioned, just like that of the First. Jesus' moral injunctions and Paul's understanding of sexuality and sexual morality dominates the Second Testament. The

Gospels contain Jesus' injunctions on marriage, divorce and adultery. Jesus, in Matthew 19:5-6, is seen affirming sexual union when he said that husband and wife become "one flesh." However, much of the Second Testament's reference to sexuality comes from Paul whose views on marriage, celibacy, and sexual immorality (problematically) still finds its place as the foundation for sexual ethics. While the biblical account of creation in the First Testament affirmed sexuality, biblical eschatology in the Second Testament contributed to a pessimistic perception of sexuality.[10] Paul's instructions to abstain from sexual pleasure, keeping in mind the second coming of Christ, has contributed to a negative perception of the body, desire and sex. That said, the presence of the eunuch in the Acts of the Apostles can be seen as an affirmation of gender fluidity.

Approaches to Understanding Sexuality

David H. Jensen offers three approaches by which the Bible has and can be used to speak of human sexuality.

a)   The Bible as a Guidebook for Sexual Behaviour

The most common way of viewing the relationship between the Bible and sexuality is in viewing the Bible as a guide for sexual behaviour. Since it offers prohibitions concerning certain sexual behaviours and acts, it can be seen as a "how-not-to" manual, although it concedes sexuality as God-given. Under this approach, sex is between a man and a woman, patterned on the model of Adam and Eve, while same-sex behaviour and sex between unmarried persons is prohibited and admonished.[11] The context and concern of the text is of little importance as what is stated in the scripture is taken to be literal, timeless and universally normative.

b)   The Bible as Oppressive on Sexuality

As some contemporary theologians have come to opine that the Bible is an insufficient, outmoded, and an oppressive guide to sexuality, Jensen suggests readers use the hermeneutic of suspicion to decipher the patriarchal notions and assumptions embedded in the text. For example, women viewed as being sexually unstable in the Pastoral Epistles and as property in the Pentateuch. Because of the patriarchal and hierarchical underpinnings, men are privileged over women and men's sexuality over that of women's.[12] As scripture is embedded in patriarchy, the use of the Bible to address sexuality under this approach is naïve and anachronistic.

c)   The Bible as a Narrative of *Eros*

Under this approach, the Bible is understood as a narrative of desire affirming the relationship between God, humans, and creation. Here, even the Bible's nonsexual texts would have something to say about sexuality. For example, the story of the woman with the hemorrhage can be understood as an act where Jesus imparts sexual healing to the woman.[13] The Bible, when read as a narrative of *eros,* offers itself as a sexual text: the Song of Songs interpreted as a sensual poem that lingers on the body, conveying touch and desire.[14] Though this is a positive approach, the reader can fall into the trap of selective reading, ignoring texts that come with an oppressive baggage.

Jensen argues that a rule-based approach is fraught with problems and it would do one good to reject it. Instead, to read the Bible as a story of God, God's being, and God's beloved would be an affirmative way of reading biblical texts.

Homosexuality and its Myths

As noted in the first chapter, the book will lay a certain emphasis on homosexuality as many Christians and churches stand divided on this very issue. A recent conversation thread in one of the newly created theological groups on Facebook revealed opinions that were polar opposite. It was disappointing, but not surprising, to see seminarians and recognised theologians condemn homosexuality as "devilish" and "satanic," claiming allegiance to the revealed morality in the Bible. In saying same-sex desire violates God's fundamental design for human relationships, these theologians and seminarians failed to overcome their heteronormative conditioning to engage in biblical abuse.

Similarly, Joseph Dias, the General Secretary of the Catholic Secular Forum, concurred in 2009, "The Church's stand on the issue has always been clear. For us it (homosexuality) is an unnatural act, against the divine law. We will definitely oppose it."[15] In 2018, after homosexuality was decriminalised in India, Stephen Fernandes, a Catholic priest, remarked, "What is legal is not equal to moral acceptability."[16] After years of protests, activism, debates, and theologising, not much has really changed. Given the obstinate posture of the Church and church-going Christians, I feel impelled to address the il/legitimacy of homosexuality.

Homosexuality is derived from two words—the Greek *homo* meaning "same" and the Latin *sexus* meaning "sex"—referring to the sexual attraction of a person to another of the same sex.[17] The term homosexuality was coined in the nineteenth century and it was during the same period that a distinction between sexual behaviour and sexual orientation was made. Later, due to medical science, homosexuality came to be viewed as a normal facet of life and not as a problem (not forgetting that medical science at one point did view it as a mental disorder.)[18] Still, even with proof from science, the Indian Church continues to perceive homosexuality as sinful, unnatural, and abnormal. In doing so, lesbians and gays are regarded as criminals under law, outcasts of society, and an abomination to religion.

Within human communities, same-sex love has always existed. In fact, same-sex behaviour has also been documented in hundreds of non-human species, from insects to animals. How then can something be called *unnatural* when it is so *natural*? The reasons why Christians attest derogatory labels to lesbians and gays is due to their outright obsession with heteronormativity and their perception of same-sex love as a violation of God's command to "be fruitful and multiply" (Genesis 1:28).

It is important to note that homosexuality, like heterosexuality, is not merely an issue of sexual activity, but primarily an issue of identity. Ethicist and scholar-activist Miguel De La Torre highlights five different myths of homosexuality that demand our attention.[19] The first myth is that homosexuality is a choice. The second myth is the reduction of the definition of homosexual identity to what is done with the genitals. The third is that homosexuality is an illness, a mental disturbance, a sin or an emotional disorder that can be cured and corrected. The fourth is in attempting to limit discussions on sexual orientations to sexual organs alone. And finally, the myth that homosexuality leads to paedophilia, literally the love for boys. These myths are still popular in our communities and regrettably people develop their attitudes towards lesbians and gays based on these myths.[20]

In a culture where heterosexuality is understood to be the only legitimate expression of sexuality, same-sex love continues to be seen as a perversion of sexuality. As Marvin Ellison points out, the subtle shifts in rendering heterosexuality from "natural" to "normal" to "normative" only illegitimates homosexuality.[21] This understanding must be contested and one way to do it is by contending same-sex desire as a legitimate and divinely ordered expression of human sexuality. A refusal to do so not only invalidates homosexuality but justifies homophobia.

There are differing views as to what the Bible says about homosexuality. Some claim the Bible is outrightly against it, while some others claim it is neither clear nor conclusive, and still others believe the Bible does affirm homoeroticism. On the surface, it is generally believed that there are seven texts, referred to as "clobber texts," that condemn or are used to condemn homosexuality.[22] While it is beyond the scope of the chapter to look at these texts individually, what is important to note in the dominant interpretations of these texts is that all these texts are stripped off their contexts, and none of them are in tune with modern-day understanding of homosexuality. Our reading of the Bible reveals much about ourselves than anything else.

One might ask why the Church does not cringe at advocating the hatred and loathing of homosexuality? The answer lies in the fact that most Christians respond to it by saying, "Homosexuality is sinful because the Bible says so" or "God said it, I believe it, that settles it," thereby pledging their allegiance to the authority of the Bible.[23] It is not surprising to hear wedding sermons emphasise heterosexual marriage and procreation as God's will. The Church, for the following reasons, repudiates same-sex relations: first, due to its understanding of purity and sexual morality; second, due to homosexual persons' inability to procreate, which is at the heart of the biblical command to marry and have sex; third, because the "Bible says so;" and fourth, because of the presumption that the patriarchal model is *the* model for all sexual relationships. These reasons are a clear reflection of the functioning of the mechanisms of biblical literalism and heteronormativity in constructing a defence of hetero-patriarchy. To leave it unattended is not just erroneous but dangerous. Acknowledging the need for such assumptions and ideologies to be critiqued, questioned, and challenged, the following sections shall state how biblical texts are read and interpreted by the LGBTQ+ members to affirm same-sex love and desire, and combat centuries of sexual violence perpetuated by hetero-patriarchal interpretations of biblical texts. The time has come to look beyond what "the Bible says" to what "the queers say."

Privileging Experience

In order to look to what "the queers say," recognising the significance of experience is crucial. Experience is considered as one of the sources of doing theology. Yet, in traditional theologising, experience is often discredited or invalidated. A queer reading, however, privileges subjective and collective experience (of exploitation, shame, oppression, love, renewal and liberation). Black queer lesbian scholar and Christian minister Pamela Lightsey, in her book *Our Lives Matter*, speaks of the importance of one's experience in understanding God, and claims that queer womanists come to understand God through their experience. Any theology that does not pay attention to the context and experience of queer persons, she declares, is a dead theology.[24]

Lightsey underlines the importance of interpreting scripture through one's experience and identity. Experience is sacred and as sexuality is a human experience, one's body-mediated experiences become imperative in doing theology. To deny the validity of the experiences of queer persons is to deny their moral sensibilities. Since experience is vital for moral reasoning, Lightsey rightfully calls Black queer womanists to claim their experience by challenging the subjection of Black queer's interpretation of scripture to "external" authority.[25] While Lightsey challenges the notion of the inherent authority of scripture, she opines that queer

Black Christian women turn to scripture for in it can be found the liberating word from the Lord.[26] Scripture, she claims, is more than a written document for queer Black women; it is a *way of life.* Lightsey writes, "We turn to the biblical witness with deep respect for its authoritative function in the churches and communities in which we worship and live."[27] Though scripture has an authoritative function, she does not hesitate to challenge the doctrine of sola scriptura and any oppressive interpretation of biblical texts. Queering the Bible entails the recentring of authority from the text to one's subjective and the community's collective experience.

In privileging experience, a reading from the margins, De La Torre states, is a reading by people in the midst of oppression.[28] This reading challenges the dominant culture, methods, and interpretations to make the text a text of hope, comfort, celebration, and one that is less harmful. Similarly, writing on Dalit engagement with the Bible, Indian theologian Sathianathan Clarke speaks of the need to *recover* the message of the Bible, and this recovery is accompanied by reading one's own subalternity—the experience of exploitation and pollution—into texts in order to validate subjectivity.[29] De La Torre, Clarke and Lightsey, all from different contexts, point to one decisive factor: the importance for oppressed communities to read and interpret scripture through their experience. They avow experience as a vital source for theologising.

The Political Tool of Queering the Bible

The study of Bible and homosexuality is not, as Ken Stone puts it, "a matter of some perspective on the topic of homosexuality [but] significantly, a matter of getting some perspective on the Bible and on biblical interpretation."[30] The Bible needs to be explored and deliberated. One way to do it is by *queering* them, i.e., making them 'strange.' The heteronormative interpretations of biblical texts accord power and privilege to those constructing them, and those using the Bible to demonise same-sex desire do so from a position of power—either by being a male or a heterosexual or both.

According to Robert Goss and Deborah Krause, queer reading is a strategy that challenges hegemonic interpretations in order to expose their heterosexist ideologies and assumptions and open them up for questioning.[31] In bridging biblical texts, contemporary concerns and subjective experiences, a queer reading allows one to find the cracks and crevices in the Bible and its contexts, displace those that are harmful, and welcome those with disruptive and "scriptive" possibilities.[32] Since multiplicity is written into texts, queer communities read their experience into the text and emerge with varied interpretations. It liberates and celebrates texts colonised by hetero-patriarchy and male chauvinism. Therefore, queering—a liberative act that subverts and eviscerates powerful and hegemonic systems that masculinise and heterosexualise the Bible—is quite simply a political tool of the queer community.

Goss identifies three reading strategies in biblical interpretation: deflecting textual violence, outing the text, and befriending the text. While the first one is a negative reading strategy, the second and third are positive and offensive reading strategies.[33] Of the third, Goss writes:

"Befriending the text is the imaginative reading from a queer social location. It does not exclude a hermeneutics of suspicion but includes a hermeneutics of queer solidarity with the marginal and perhaps more importantly a hermeneutics of queer imagination. It can include a hermeneutics of queer eroticism...."[34]

In the above quote, Goss makes reference to several hermeneutical approaches such as hermeneutics of queer eroticism, hermeneutics of suspicion, hermeneutics of queer solidarity, and hermeneutics of queer imagination. But the precondition for its usage is one's queer social location. Thus, the social location of the interpreter *is* crucial.

Primacy of Social Location

Homosexuality is condemned as the readers conveniently reside in and speak from the centre, deriving power and privilege from the same.[35] Their social location allows them to be complicit with sexism and homophobia.[36] Likewise, a reader who is located socially within the collective of the LGBTQ+ community produces a queer reading of the Bible. Ken Stone and Mona West argue that the social location of the reader is vital in this political process.[37] To read from one's social location not only involves reading from their geographical position, i.e., from the margins, but also reading from their bodies and varied sexual orientations.[38] Another term that West uses for social location is "community situation approach," which, according to her, refers to the community's social history of oppression, justified by the mis/use of the Bible.[39] The subversion of hegemonic interpretations, Lisa Isherwood and Elizabeth Stuart note, is increasingly possible when the agents of subversion are the furthest away from the centre of dominating power.[40] If the ones at the periphery are to be taken seriously, the centre must be spoken to.[41]

Queering the Doctrine of Sin

Since queers have grown up being labelled as sinners owing to their sexual orientations and preferences, queer theologians and thinkers have resorted to interpret the doctrine of sin in different ways. Robert Williams, a gay priest, argues it is not a sin to be a homosexual. Instead, sin is the rejection of oneself (or, in other words, a homosexual's desire to be 'straight').[42] In India, as in other countries, lesbians and gays are given in marriage (by their parents) to persons of the opposite sex with the hope that this new alliance would cure their homosexualness. Opposing this method of 'cure', Henri, one of Joseph N. Goh's interviewees, states that "actively participating in that lie would be a sin."[43] To sin, Goh writes, "is to reject the knowledge of one's desire."[44] Therefore, rejecting one's desires and uniting with a person of the opposite sex is to dishonour God and the individual. It is clear from the above statements that homosexual identity is not understood as a sin, but rather the rejection of that identity, of that sexual desire, as a sin against God and neighbour.

Some have embraced the traditional concept of original sin as being a "radical equaliser"—meaning no one is exempt from the clutches of original sin. Such an understanding dissolves the boundaries of morally good and morally bad people. Some others have tried to preserve the doctrine of sin by focusing on systemic and societal sin. Here, the focus is shifted from particular sexual acts or individual sins to structural foundations of oppression and exploitation. This perspective views sexism, racism, casteism and heterosexism as sins.

Cheng further proposes an alternate reading of sin—sin as essentialism or the rejection of radical love. Here God/Christ is understood as a love that dissolves existing boundaries (sexual and gender), and the rejection of this radical love is sin. [45] While traditionally sin has been viewed as a crime against God that deserves punishment, Cheng urges the Christian community to do away with this crime-based model and embrace the Christ-centred model where sin is understood as a temporary phase of immaturity or incomplete growth as one is always moving to attain the ultimate goal, i.e., to be made divine in the image of Christ.[46]

In her recent essay, "God in Dirty Places: Filthy Love and a Wrestling God," Priscilla Rawade expresses her friend's interpretation of sin that I think deserves attention. Her friend says,

> "Sin is when you belittle people and are deaf to their stories because of your all-knowing ego. Sin is you, using God's word to create hate and fear for people who are different, as they do not serve your patriarchal structures. Sin is your hearts of stone, which is stubborn not to understand that love has to be the center in our quest for God. Sin is you being arrogant and dismissive not to accept [the] life in abundance, which Christ promised…"[47]

This understanding of sin points to the dangers in violating the neighbour through manifestations of ego, arrogance, indifference, hate and fear. In violating the neighbour, one ends up violating Christ. Rawade's friends' naming of sins—such as ego, hate, fear, stubbornness and arrogance—do not insulate systems of oppressions such as patriarchy, sexism and homophobia, but rather places value on how individual acts, innocent as they might seem in private conversations, have the potential to contribute to social systems of injustice.[48] Her naming of sins also points to how social systems in turn influence our understanding of sin.

In a living tradition, doctrines, forming part of a long tradition in Christianity, are vital for the faith of communities. Recognising that doctrines are historically constructed by heterosexual men with privilege and power, the task of reinterpreting them become indispensable. In queering texts and doctrines that have otherwise been prejudicial, the LGBTQ+ community see themselves as agents who have 'come out' to expose the sins of the 'straight' community. Queering scripture, doctrines and traditions allow queer communities to theologise from their social location and experience. In doing so they not only embrace the subversity of Christian faith but also, and importantly, celebrate their sexualities. Narratives of and from queer bodies are needed to transform our histories.

Endnotes

[1] Sexual ethics concerns issues regarding sexuality, including sexual behaviour. It relates to community and personal standards of conduct in interpersonal relations, sexual relations, issues of power and consent, and how individual behaviour aspects impacts society. See, Presbyterian Church of Aotearoa New Zealand, *Sexual Ethics* (Wellington: Presbyterian Church of Aotearoa New Zealand), 5. While traditional sexual ethics, characterised by codes of control, inequality and violence, catered to the sexual practices of heterosexuals alone, Kevin Kelly states that sexual ethics become ethical and liberative for all when it espouses human freedom, friendship, intimacy, love, goodness of human body and sensual joy, and uniqueness of human person and personal conscience. See, Kevin T. Kelly, *New Directions in*

Sexual Ethics: Moral Theology and the Challenge of AIDS (London: Geoffrey Chapman, 1998), 139.

[2] David M. Carr, *The Erotic Word. Sexuality, Spirituality and the Bible* (New York: Oxford University Press, 2003), 3.

[3] Miguel A. De La Torre, *A Lily among the Thorns: Imagining a New Christian Sexuality* (San Francisco: John Wiley & Sons, 2007), 1.

[4] J. Harold Ellens, *Sex in the Bible. A New Consideration* (London: Praeger, 2006), 9.

[5] Anthony Kosnik, et al., *Human Sexuality: New Directions in American Catholic Thought* (New York: Paulist Press, 1977), 10.

[6] Anthony Kosnik, et al., *Human Sexuality: New Directions in American Catholic Thought*, 17.

[7] J. Harold Ellens, *Sex in the Bible. A New Consideration*, 15.

[8] David M. Carr, *The Erotic Word. Sexuality, Spirituality and the Bible*, 171.

[9] Georvin Joseph, "Human Sexuality as a Garden of Celebrations," in *Public and Sensual: Exploring Solutions. Bible Studies on Human Sexuality*, ed. Christopher Rajkumar (Nagpur: NCCI, 2012), 75-76.

[10] Anthony Kosnik, et al., *Human Sexuality: New Directions in American Catholic Thought*, 29.

[11] David H. Jensen, "The Bible and Sex," in *The Embrace of Eros: Bodies, Desires, and Sexuality in Christianity*, ed. Margaret D. Kamitsuka (Minneapolis: Fortress Press, 2010), 16-17.

[12] David H. Jensen, "The Bible and Sex," 20-21.

[13] David H. Jensen, "The Bible and Sex," 24.

[14] David H. Jensen, "The Bible and Sex," 27.

[15] Rahul Benjamin, "Church to oppose legalization of gay sex in India," *Christian Today*, http://www.christiantoday.co.in/article/church.to.oppose. legalization.of.gay.sex.in.india/4118.htm (accessed July 19, 2019).

[16] Bijay Kumar Minj, "India Church unhappy with legalization of homosexuality," *UCA News*, https://www.ucanews.com/news/india-church-unhappy-with-legalization-of-homosexuality/83280 (accessed June 8, 2020).

[17] Peter Coleman, *Christian Attitudes to Homo-sexuality* (London: SPCK, 1980), 4-5.

[18] The official declaration of homosexuality as a variant of human sexuality was passed by the American Psychiatric Association in 1973 and the World Health Organization in 1992. See, Judith K. Balswick and Jack O. Balswick, *Authentic Human Sexuality: An Integrated Christian Approach*, 2nd ed. (Illinois: InterVarsity Press, 2008), 95.

[19] Miguel A. De La Torre, *A Lily among the Thorns: Imagining a New Christian Sexuality*, 134-138.

[20] In the Indian context, some movies have been pro-homosexuality. But even they, for comical purposes, portray gay men as those who randomly exchange sensual looks at other men underlining the assumption that gay men lack the ability for faithful and genuine relationships, and so engage in random flirtation with members of the same-sex. Ashley Tellis argues that Hindi films have projected homosexuals as "classic commodified appropriations of the 'cool,'" and these representations quite rightly do not engage with the "subjectivities of same-sex subjects." See, Ashley Tellis, "The politics of cinematic visibility," *DNA*, http://www.dnaindia.com/lifestyle/report-the-politics-of-cinematic-visibility-1676028 (accessed June 6, 2020). Furthermore, the practice of "curing" lesbians and gays by marrying them off to the opposite sex is still prevalent in India.

[21] Marvin M. Ellison, *Erotic Justice: A Liberation Ethic of Sexuality*, 33.

[22] Genesis 19, Jude 7, Leviticus 18:22, Leviticus 20:13, Romans 1:21-28, 1 Corinthians 6:9-10, and 1 Timothy 1:10. As already noted elsewhere, the biblical authors had no knowledge of homosexuality as a sexual orientation but only as sexual acts.

[23] The second phrase is borrowed from John Corvino.

[24] Pamela Lightsey, *Our Lives Matter: A Womanist Queer Theology* (Wipf and Stock Publishers, 2015), 37.

[25] Pamela Lightsey, *Our Lives Matter*, 44.

[26] Pamela Lightsey, *Our Lives Matter*, 39.

[27] Pamela Lightsey, *Our Lives Matter*, 39.

[28] Miguel A. De La Torre, *Reading the Bible from the Margins* (New York: Orbis Books, 2003), 4.

[29] Sathianathan Clarke, "Viewing the Bible Through the Eyes and Ears of Subalterns in India," *Biblical Interpretation*, 10:3 (2002): 259. https://brill.com/abstract/journals/bi/10/3/article-p245_2.xml (accessed June 13, 2020).

[30] Ken Stone, "What the Homosexuality Debates Really Say about the Bible," in *Out of the Shadows into the Light: Christianity and Homosexuality*, ed. Miguel A. De La Torre (St. Louis: Chalice Press, 2009), 23.

[31] Robert E. Goss and Deborah Krause, "The Pastoral Letters: 1 and 2 Timothy, and Titus," *The Queer Bible Commentary*, Deryn Guest, et.al (London: SCM Press, 2006), 684.

[32] Ellen T. Armour, "Queer Bibles, Queer Scriptures? An Introductory Response," *Bible Trouble. Queer Readings at the Boundaries of Biblical Scholarship*, eds. Teresa J. Hornsby and Ken Stone (Atlanta: Society of Biblical Literature, 2011), 6.

[33] Robert E. Goss, *Queering Christ: Beyond Jesus Acted Up* (Cleveland: The Pilgrim Press, 2002), 205-206. Befriending the text strategy has been used to unearth queer identities like David, Jonathan, Ruth, Naomi, and the unnamed gay Centurion in Luke 7.

[34] Robert E. Goss, *Queering Christ,* 217.

[35] When one speaks of social location, the question of margin-centre framework arises. I use the word "margin" to refer to the exploited and oppressed communities that are distant from the power and privilege of the centre. Patrick Cheng states that queer theology would bring those at the margins to the centre. (Note his use of the margin-centre category.) While I disagree on the movement from the margins to the centre, on terms that a mere reversal of this hierarchy or pattern of interaction would not challenge the heteronormative system but end up perpetuating it, I defend Cheng's use of the margin-centre category when it comes to recognising the social location of the reader. The margin-centre framework is often accused of being constructed and enforced by the dominant. Should one then refrain from using this framework? If the framework is dissolved, one must ask the question as to how members of the LGBTQ+ community would express themselves. After all is it not within the web of differences do patterns of meaning emerge? If one uses this margin-centre category with its political implications, it does makes sense. The suggestion to do away with it only suits the agenda of the centre. Doing away with the framework is in a way calling for a negation of differences, which on the other hand is essential to those at the margins. Therefore, the discourse of margin and centre is a strategic and a political tool of the ones occupying the margins. A queer reading may bring those at the margins to the centre as Cheng asserts, but even if it does not, it certainly affirms the location, voice and experience of the margin-alised.

[36] Homophobia can be understood as the irrational fear and hatred of lesbians and gays.

[37] Ken Stone, "Queer Commentary and Biblical Interpretation: An Introduction," in *Queer Commentary and the Hebrew Bible,* ed. Ken Stone (Ohio: The Pilgrim Press, 2001), 19.

[38] Thomas Bohache, *Christology from the Margins* (London: SCM Press, 2008), 207.

[39] Mona West, "Shaped by the Word," in *Out of the Shadows into the Light: Christianity and Homosexuality,* ed. Miguel A. De La Torre (St. Louis: Chalice Press, 2009), 82.

[40] Lisa Isherwood and Elizabeth Stuart, *Introducing Body Theology* (Sheffield: Sheffield Academic Press, 1998), 100.

[41] Miguel A. De La Torre, *Latina/o Social Ethics: Moving Beyond Eurocentric Moral Thinking* (Texas: Baylor University Press, 2010), 5.

[42] Robert Williams, *Just as I Am: A Practical Guide to being Out, Proud and Christian* (New York: Harper Perennial, 1992), 151. Cited in, Patrick S. Cheng, *From Sin to Amazing Grace: Discovering the Queer Christ* (New York: Seabury Books, 2012), 9.

[43] Joseph N. Goh, *Living Out Sexuality and Faith: Body Admissions of Malaysian Gay and Bisexual Men* (New York: Routledge, 2018), 131.

[44] Joseph N. Goh, *Living Out Sexuality and Faith,* 131.

[45] Patrick S. Cheng, *An Introduction to Queer Theology: Radical Love* (New York: Seabury Books, 2011), 72-74.

[46] Patrick S. Cheng, *From Sin to Amazing Grace: Discovering the Queer Christ* (New York: Seabury Books, 2012), xii-xiii.

[47] Priscilla Rawade, "God in Dirty Places: Filthy Love and a Wrestling God," *God in Dirty Places,* https://gindp.blogspot.com/2020/06/day-24-god-in-dirty-places-filthy-love.html (accessed on June 13, 2020).

[48] Theodore W. Jennings Jr., "Reconstructing the Doctrine of Sin," in *The Other Side of Sin: Woundedness from the Perspective of the Sinned-Against,* eds. Andrew Sung Park and Susan L. Nelson (Albany: State University of New York Press, 2001), 113.

3

The Body and Safe Spirituality

When engaging with human sexuality, one cannot bypass the significance of the body. The body throughout centuries has been viewed negatively—as against the spirit—making the body a site of sinful pleasures. Within early Christian history, much was spoken and written on the creation of the body, disciplining the body, sanctifying the body, healing of the body, and death of the body, but the human body as a sexual body was less discussed and far from being affirmed. Since body and sexuality are interconnected, it is important to restore the body as a sexual body within a theological framework. To this end, the chapter will offer perspectives affirming the body and its pleasures. It will also explore the interconnectedness between sexuality and spirituality, which has been long neglected.

The Predicament of Dualism

One of the reasons for a low valuation of the body and its pleasures is the dualistic binary that pervades much of Christian thought.[1] Nelson defines dualism as "the sense of two different elements which may live together in an uneasy truce but are frequently in conflict."[2] Dualism—the separation of body and soul—results in the marginalisation of the body and its passions. Adrian Thatcher rightly points out that the problem in viewing sexuality under dualism is that it fails to be celebrated, instead becoming "the occasion of God's judgment."[3] Therefore, in the words of Elaine Storkey, "Dualism… is the enemy… of authentic Christianity,"[4] as it is unbiblical and ends up vandalising human bodies.

Sylvia Thorson-Smith, writing on sexuality and dualism, says there are two primary forms of dualism: spiritual dualism and sexual dualism. Spiritual dualism primarily refers to the body/soul binary while the latter implies male/female, homosexual/heterosexual, and masculinity/femininity.[5] As dualism invests power, value, and privilege to some categories over others, the enforcement of white privilege, male prerogative, caste power, and heterosexual supremacy has caused much harm to sexuality and the human body. Because dualisms perpetuate prejudice and catalogues sexuality into "dos and don'ts," Butler calls for the erasure of these dualistic binary oppositions, affirming the indeterminacy and instability of all sexed and gendered identities.[6]

In traditional epistemology, knowledge had to spring up from the mind. René Descartes is known to have made the mind the locus of knowledge and the body a mere mechanical system of muscles.[7] The body (and its experiences) was seen as an obstacle to rational and intellectual thought.[8] But if sexuality is a human experience, then experience is vital to fruitful living. Experience is both personal and communal, and one must be sensitive to regard its ability to form moral discernment. Elizabeth Grosz speaks of the embodied self as the knower where subjective experiences are taken into account.[9] Likewise, for lesbians and gays, Lisa Isherwood avows, bodily desires and experiences aid in their process of "coming out." This implies that knowing the truth about their own bodies is what sets them free.[10] Since the lived experiences of persons and communities function as a form of agency and resistance, affirming the body-mediated experiences of people is deeply significant.

Sinful Depraved Body to Sexual Erotic Body

Too often the Church has treated the body as a source of problems (illness, disability, lust, violence, etc.) and not as a source of pleasure and sensuality.[11] Pleasure is considered only to be a result of sexual activities and not as an intrinsic purpose of sex. Persons are defined by their desires and what they do with their bodies in order to fulfil those desires. Their bodies lie in bondage to the expectations of the Church and society which forever are in want to discipline it. If sexuality is a justice issue, violation of the body and denial of body right must be perceived as an issue of sexual injustice.[12]

Within the Brahmanical culture, Gavin Flood opines, the body is seen as impure and this negative view of the body and of sexuality is deeply connected to an environment that is misogynistic.[13] Winnie Varghese, an Episcopal priest, categorically states that colonialism and the "consumer/consumptive/aspirational culture" formed the Indian body.[14] Additionally, Nelson writes, "When the body is experienced as a *thing,* it has the right to live only as machine or slave owned by the self."[15] These observations imply that the body's significance rests in one's ability to control and restrict it. The body is feared, deprived of *eros*, and alienated within the self and from God. Not to mention how the body is seen as mortal and carnal as against the spirit that is immortal and spiritual. This reverberates the hetero-patriarchal logic that governs dualistic thinking, where the body becomes a transitory machine in need of constant monitoring and disciplining.

One of the main contributions of feminist and lesbian thinkers in the field of sexual ethics is the recognition of the erotic that serves as a context and as a substitute for certain sexual practices. Therefore, standing in contrast to the demonisation of the body is a theological position that welcomes the body and its sensations as a sexual and erotic instrument needed for understanding the self, the world, and God. It accords power, in this case "erotic power," to the body allowing it to function as a sexual instrument. Speaking on the eroticising power of the body, Ellison states that this erotic energy is ethical when it is experienced between two bodies with a sense of freedom, respect, playfulness, and intimacy (and two bodies can imply same-sexed as well).[16] It is important to allow individuals to discover their own means and ideas of the erotic through their bodily experiences. Dualistic thought has forced people to repress their sexual needs and channelise them only towards members of the opposite sex. But to issue a blueprint for such a course is to limit the diverse s/expressions of the body. For the body to assume its potentialities as a sexual erotic body, it needs to escape the phenomenon of normalisation as normalisation restricts the body from journeying the path of erotic pleasure and self-discovery.

Who defines lesbian and gay sexual desire? Who defines trans passions and queer love? Why should sexual desire function within a continuum of heterosexist norms when it has the (erotic) power to carve out its own sexual journey? These are questions queer bodies ask and it is imperative that the Church comes to understand and respect the fluid nature of bodily sensations, erotic expressions and fulfilments. Eugene Rogers states affirmatively that "[T]he movement of *eros* is first of all a reflection, in their bodies, of the love God has for human beings."[17] If the human body negates its erotic passions, it misses out on mirroring God's erotic love as a response to God and as a covenant to another individual.

Analysing the Sexuality-Spirituality Nexus of Victorian Morality

I deal with the topic in this chapter as I believe the Victorian construction of sexual morality has had a deep influence on Christian spirituality. And as we are exploring the connection between the two, I find it relevant to expose the sexuality-spirituality connection that British colonialism brought to our land.

The Victorian era, ideologically and historically identified with the reign of Queen Victoria in England, was characterised by a high degree of moral strictness consisting of hard work, sexual repression, responsibility, prudery, and social hierarchy. Strong emphasis was laid on the control of sexuality (especially that of women) as a means of maintaining social and cultural order. It viewed desire and pleasure as impediments to salvation and viewed the body negatively. As the society was deeply patriarchal, family values had to be adhered to and sexuality was used as a tool to define and control individuals.[18] Gladson Jathanna mentions how men, during the Victorian age, had access to the public sphere, while women were relegated to the private. This is indicative of a clear binary between "sexually active" men and "sexually passive" women.[19] Homosexuality and other forms of sexual practices and sexual acts were deemed illegal and gross. As Victorian morality was deeply influenced by evangelical movements such as Evangelical Awakenings, Pietism and Puritanism, Christianity certainly had a dominant role to play in the creation of a sexually repressive culture. As the moral behaviour of the people were ordered by the moral codes prescribed by the empire, an austere spirituality was the eventual outcome.

Sensing the need to place the understanding of sexuality within the trajectory of colonialism, theologian and ethicist George Zachariah states how the British were inspired by the "deontological call of civilizing the heathens," and so identified customs and practices that were immoral to them.[20] The sexualities they encountered in India were considered 'uncivilised' and so began the process of civilising the natives. Because of the influence of Victorian morality and the normative Judeo-Christian understanding of sexual morality, they sought to control, colonise and criminalise the Indian body. Probing further, Zachariah states that such a provision granted power to the state to intervene in, colonise and intrude into the private and intimate spaces of persons, especially the ones lacking legal standing.[21] It ended up categorising sexual acts as natural and unnatural, placing those deemed unnatural at the bottom of the sexual hierarchy.[22] This process of moralising sexual desires and behaviours affected and governed the spirituality of Indians, particularly Christians, just as it did the British themselves.

Ensuring Safe Spirituality

Ellison's essay "Practicing Safer Spirituality" inspirits the above subheading and the title of the chapter. We have heard the mantra "safe sex" through advertisements and campaigns. Yet, as spirituality is deeply intertwined with sexuality, it is important to take care, guard and practice safe spirituality. If spirituality is part of being human, so is sexuality. This makes us spiritual beings and sexual beings. The two are not to be seen as opposites for each affects the other. Toinette Eugene defines spirituality as "the human capacity to be self-transcending, relational, and freely committed, encompasses all of life, including our human sexuality."[23] Of the connection between the two, Raymond J. Lawrence writes:

> When the central energy of our inherent vitality expresses itself in a transcendent reach for meaning and connection, through our psyches, toward God, we call it spirituality. When that same force expresses itself horizontally through our psyches and bodies toward another human, we call it sexuality. It is the same force. Healthy sexuality and spirituality are inseparable.[24]

Inseparable they are! The above quote, like Eugene's statement, is suggestive of the interconnectedness between our spirituality and sexuality. To distort one is to distort the other. Kelly Brown

Douglas rightly states, "To be estranged from one's sexuality in all of its dimensions portends a diminished relationship with God."[25] Far too often, Christianity has sought to control the sexualities of people, particularly those at the margins, thereby distorting their spiritualities and their relationships with the divine. This, according to Karen Lebacqz and Joseph Driskill, is unsafe spirituality. Unsafe spirituality leads to spiritual abuse. Spiritual abuse, they say, occurs "whenever someone's sense of self or connection to God (their 'spiritual empowerment') is weakened, undermined, or decreased." When the Church calls people's sexualities into question by imposing heterosexist definitions upon them and thwarting them from relating to the divine in their own nonconformist ways, the Church abuses people, spiritually and sexually. The Church, in this way, places undue spiritual burdens on queer subjects. It persists in identifying homosexuality, bisexuality, transgenderism, masturbation, anal sex, and sex outside marriage as sexual sins. No wonder that fear, suspicion and hatred encompass any discourse on sex,[26] resulting in sex-negativity and creating feelings of guilt and shame in people (it is for this reason I am convinced that even guilt and shame are social constructs). The Church, in sexually and spiritually abusing queer people, dismembers them from the body of Christ.

A hetero-patriarchal understanding of sexuality, modelled after Victorian morality and spirituality, grants privilege and power to heterosexuals, thereby validating their form of spirituality as against other forms that are governed and modelled after a body-affirming, sex-positive ethic. The compulsory enforcement of heterosexuality needs to be confronted to bring about safe spirituality. To bring about safe spirituality, heterosexuals need to recognise the wonder in queer persons and affirm their desires, vulnerabilities, and needs. Fear and hatred (of diversity and difference) need to be undone, and the Church needs to abandon the oppressive theology it has held dear for centuries together. If we continue to hold on to exclusive theologies where persons different to us are excluded from participating in the life of the Church and faith communities, we grant credence to violence, shame, oppression, division, hate, prejudice, and (spiritual) abuse. Douglas reminds us that there can be "… no excuse for placing a sacred canopy over any type of injustice or human misery…"[27] Injustices of all kinds have to be eliminated to ensure a safe spirituality so that everyone can feel safe with the/ir idea of the divine.

Endnotes

[1] Somen Das remarks that a low valuation of body was present in certain aspects of classical Hindu thought as well. This suggests that the body was perceived as sinful within the Christian faith and also within an Indian culture that is dominated by Hindu thought. See, Somen Das, *Christian Ethics and Indian Ethos* (New Delhi: ISPCK, 1994), 13.

[2] James B. Nelson, *Embodiment: An Approach to Sexuality and Christian Theology*, 37.

[3] Adrian Thatcher, *Liberation Sex: A Christian Sexual Theology* (London: SPCK, 1993), 31.

[4] Elaine Storkey, "Sex and Sexuality in the Church," in *Mirror to the Church: Reflections on* Sexism (London: SPCK, 1988), 52. Cited in, Adrian Thatcher, *Liberation Sex: A Christian Sexual Theology*, 33.

[5] Sylvia Thorson-Smith, "Becoming 'Possessed: Toward Sexual Health and Well-Being,'" in *Body and Soul: Rethinking Sexuality as Justice-Love*, eds. Marvin M. Ellison and Sylvia Thorson-Smith (Oregon: Wipf & Stock, 2003), 238.

[6] While addressing dualism, it is important to address the problem of gender binaries and the fluidity of gender identities. Gender binary or

binarism is a classification of sex and gender into two opposite and distinct categories of masculine and feminine. Transpersons, however, do not fall into these demarked categories. They transcend the dualist gender binary system and this is regarded as the epitome of identity deconstruction. However, if a transperson identifies with any particular gender it does not mean that the person validates the binary system. As Kate Bornstein points out, it could be a desire for transformation where desire itself is a transformative activity. See, Kate Bornstein, *Gender Outlaws* (New York: Routledge, 1994), 120. Cited in, Judith Butler, *Undoing Gender* (New York: Routledge, 2004), 8. The point is that though these gender binaries exist, transpersons transcend these boundaries and negate the dominance and influence these categories have in defining them.

[7] Richard M. Zaher, "Embodiment: The Phenomenological Tradition," in *Encyclopedia of Bioethics,* ed. Warren Thomas Reich, rev. ed. (New York: Simon & Schuster Macmillan, 1995), 291. Cited in, Margaret A. Farley, *Just Love: A Framework for Christian Sexual Ethics,* 112.

[8] In India, homosexuality and transgenderism are still understood as a medical disorder that needs treatment. Therefore, the link between body as the locus of knowledge and the queer person's intellectual inability perfectly suits the interests of a hetero-patriarchal society.

[9] Elizabeth Grosz, "Bodies and Knowledges: Feminism and the Crisis of Reason," in *Feminist Epistemologies*, eds. Linda Alcoff and Elizabeth Potter (New York: Routledge, 1993), 198-199. Cited in, Esther Parajuli, *Sensuous Bodies and Sensuous Texts: Towards a Feminist Theological Understanding of Human Sexuality* (M.Th. Thesis: Senate of Serampore, 2014), 35.

[10] Lisa Isherwood and Elizabeth Stuart, *Introducing Body Theology* (Sheffield: Sheffield Academic Press, 1998), 98. *Eros* is the desire to know and to be known and so the erotic body communicates that same desire. If *eros* is divine, so is the erotic body. Joseph Prabhakar Dayam, "Towards a Liberatory Christian Theology for Men: Interrogating the Gendered Self," in *Created in God's Image: From Hegemony to Partnership,* eds. Patricia Sheerattan-Bisnauth and Philip Vinod Peacock (Geneva: WCC, 2010), 79.

[11] Davina Cooper, "Speaking beyond thinking: Citizenship, governance and lesbian and gay politics," in *Sexuality and the Law: Feminist Engagements,* eds. Vanessa E. Munro and Carl F. Stychin (New York: Routledge-Cavendish, 2007), 184.

[12] Marvin M. Ellison, *Erotic Justice: A Liberating Ethic of Sexuality,* 40.

[13] Gavin Flood, *The Tantric Body: The Secret Tradition of Hindu Religion* (New York: I.B. Tauris & Co. Ltd., 2006), 39-40.

[14] Winnie Varghese, "Eliminating Homophobia in the Indian Church: The Goodness of the Body," in *Disruptive Faith, Inclusive Communities: Church and Homophobia*, eds. George Zachariah and Vincent Rajkumar (Bangalore/Delhi: CISRS/ISPCK, 2015), 225.

[15] James B. Nelson, *Embodiment*, 41.

[16] Marvin M. Ellison, *Erotic Justice: A Liberation Ethic of Sexuality*, 80.

[17] Eugene F. Rogers, Jr., *Sexuality and the Christian Body: Their Way into the Triune God* (Massachusetts: Blackwell Publishers Ltd., 1999), 232.

[18] Dennis Grube, *At the Margins of Victorian Britain: Politics, Immorality and Britishness in the Nineteenth Century* (London: I.B. Tauris & Co Ltd., 2013), 127-128.

[19] Gladson Jathanna, "Victorian Morality and Colonization of the Body in Missionary Discourse," in *A Theological Reader on Human Sexuality and Gender Diversities: Envisioning Inclusivity*, eds. Roger Gaikward and Thomas Ninan (Delhi/Nagpur: ISPCK/NCCI, 2017), 122.

[20] George Zachariah, "Introduction," in *Disruptive Faith, Inclusive Communities: Church and Homophobia*, eds. George Zachariah and Vincent Rajkumar (Bangalore/Delhi: CISRS/ISPCK, 2015), xvii-xviii.

[21] George Zachariah, "Introduction," in *Disruptive Faith, Inclusive Communities: Church and Homophobia*, xvii-xviii.

[22] Arvind Narrain, "Queering Democracy," in *Law Like Love: Queer Perspectives on Law*, eds., Arvind Narrain and Alok Gupta (New Delhi: Yoda Press, 2011), 17.

[23] Toinette Eugene, "While Love is Unfashionable: Ethical Implications of Black Spirituality and Sexuality," in *Sexuality and the Sacred: Sources for Theological Reflection*, eds. James B. Nelson and Sandra P. Longfellow (Louisville: Westminster/John Knox Press, 1994), 108-109.

[24] Raymond J. Lawrence, Jr., *Sexual Liberation: The Scandal of Christendom* (Connecticut: Praeger, Publishers, 2007), xi.

[25] Kelly Brown Douglas, *Sexuality and the Black Church: A Womanist Perspective* (Maryknoll: Orbis Books, 2004), 84-85.

[26] Marvin M. Ellison, "Practicing Safer Spirituality: Changing the Subject and Focusing on Justice," in *Out of the Shadows into the Light: Christianity and Homosexuality*, ed. Miguel A. De La Torre (St. Louis: Chalice Press, 2009), 2-3.

[27] Kelly Brown Douglas, *Sexuality and the Black Church*, 91.

4

Marriage, Family, and Homo/Sexuality

Homosexuality or same-sex attraction is often perceived to be a threat to marriage and family. Rather than seeing same-sex relations as an opportunity to redefine marriage and family, conservative Christians deem this form of relationship as undermining and desacralising the biblical understanding of marriage, which is between a man and a woman, and the family, which has the male as its head. In this chapter, I problematise homophobia before offering a critique of the heterosexed institution of marriage and family. Christians often tend to conceal their homophobic prejudices in the garb of advocating the protection of "family values," forgetting that the two are very much linked. In conclusion, I mention why same-sex relationships can be viewed as a promise rather than a threat to marriage and family.

Problematising Homophobia

The invention of the word homophobia is attributed to George Weinberg back in the 1970's. To him, homophobia was a form of prejudice. He writes, "… the phobia appears as antagonism directly toward a particular group of people. Inevitably, it leads to disdain toward the people themselves, and to mistreatment of them."[1] Homophobia can be understood as the irrational fear and hatred of lesbians and gays. It implies discrimination in all forms against them and does not necessarily imply fear in a psychiatric sense.[2] Its effects can range from silence at the sight of injustice to verbal threats, physical abuse and murder. Because of homophobia, homosexuals, and not just homosexual behaviour, are considered deviant.[3] This makes homophobia a systemic political retaliation against lesbians and gays.

Homophobia has two sides to it: the internal (not internalised homophobia) and the external. Butler states that the heterosexual's refusal to acknowledge the primary homosexual attachment in oneself is culturally enforced by a prohibition of homosexuality. Further in her analysis, she argues that a heterosexual male needs a woman as an object to prove that he never felt homosexual desire or never grieved over the loss of such desire.[4] Writing on masculinity as homophobia, Michael Kimmel makes a similar assertion when he says, "homophobia is... the fear that we might be perceived as gay."[5] This suggests that heterosexuals, particularly men, tend to possess the fear of being homosexual themselves. Monnica Williams, a clinical psychologist, calls it "homosexuality anxiety."[6] Gregory M. Herek seems to have taken the idea further in stating that (psychological) homophobia is a rejection of one's own homoerotic desires. He calls this a conflict of "me versus myself."[7] And so, homophobia should not be understood merely as loathing towards lesbians and gays but also as the fear of being a homosexual. However, as Christian gay activist Romal Laisram asserts, this need not be the case with all heterosexual persons.[8] Whether the above analyses be true or not, my point is that in most, if not all, modern discourses on sexuality, only one aspect of homophobia—the irrational fear of homosexuals or "me versus them"—is given primacy while the other is ignored.

According to Varghese, homophobia is not natural; it is a social construct.[9] Interestingly, she also sees the connection between patriarchy and homophobia as it embodies violence and social control over the sexual freedom and legal rights of lesbians and gays. Patriarchy needs heterosexuality for its survival and heterosexuality needs homophobia for its ascendency over other forms of sexual preferences.[10] When homophobia, having its roots in heterosexism, is enforced by it and works along with patriarchy, it functions as a paradigm of oppression. Can homophobia then be adjudged as sin?

Homophobia as Sin

Varghese finds homophobia to be theologically and biblically erroneous as it violates the gospel's cry for freedom. For her, Jesus is freedom and Paul's words in Galatians echoes freedom: "It is for freedom that Christ has set us free."[11] Today, the word freedom has become a cliché because oppression has become so normal. But it is important to remember that the theme is central to the gospel and indelible to human beings. 1 John 4:18 says, "There is no fear in love, but perfect love casts out fear…" If homophobia is defined as a fear of lesbians and gays, it clearly violates the character of love. Perhaps, this is why Divya, a bisexual and a believer, sees homophobia as sin as it distorts God's command to love unconditionally.[12] Jesus was never threatened or repelled by people around him. Though society saw some as a threat to the purity of the social and religious order, nothing prevented Jesus from entering into a relationship with them. Being homophobic causes one to refrain from relating to others and be like the Pharisee in the Gospel who prayed, "God, I thank you that I am not like other people."[13] Just the way he saw himself being morally superior to thieves, rouges, adulterers, and the tax collector, homophobia makes one see others as more depraved than oneself.[14] Is it not sinful to have this self-righteous attitude?

Christian Theology of Marriage and Family

Much has been made about homosexuality dismantling the (biblical) concept of marriage and family. This section seeks to address that concern. While the Church might come to agree that homophobia is wrong and homosexuality is another form of sexual expression, it could be done in the garb of preserving and privileging heterosexual family and marriage. As Zachariah points out, one of the main criticisms against homosexuality is its potential to threaten the existing dominant family system.[15] Before I respond to this conventional viewpoint held by most Christians, a word on the Christian theology of marriage and family seems appropriate. A survey of Christian theology of marriage, as you would soon notice, is nothing but a review of a patriarchal history of marriage.

Traditional family system is the bulwark of patriarchy and heterosexism and marriage is one of the most revered cultural institutions. (It is also a political and an economic institution.)

Within this system of institutionalised relationship, it is not hard to find how heterosexism and sexism continue to operate, with religious justifications. For this reason, marriage alongside a theology that ignores or justifies unjust power relations and gender and sexual oppression, respectively, need to be interrogated.

Writing on sex and marriage, Mark Jordan argues that "Christian theology not only restricts sex to marriage, it restricts sex within marriage."[16] In other words, marriage alone provides a space for sex, and only for certain forms of sexual acts to be expressed. Drawing from Augustine's *On the Good of Marriage,* Jordan lists four criteria that must be met between husband and wife. First, marriage must be monogamous and permanent; second, marriage must allow reproduction; third, the criterion of obligation demands partners accept "reasonable requests for sexual intercourse"; and finally, the criterion of temperance implies that the couple should not indulge in excessive sexual activity.[17] These criteria provide us a general overlay of how Christians and the Church think of marriage and family even today.

Christian theology of marriage is not founded on the theological formulations of Augustine alone. Clement of Alexandria, Martin Luther and John Calvin also had something to say of marriage and the permissibility of sexual expression within the bounds of marriage. Clement is known to have emphasised on the virtue of self-control, while stating that sexual intercourse was strictly for married people, i.e., between a man and a woman. He also understands semen, the product of the male sexual organ, to be the only principle of generation, highlighting the impure and subordinated status of women.[18] For Luther, marriage is between the male and the female, and since marriage redeems sex, it is only for married couples. Sex outside marriage was demonic and coarse.[19] Likewise for Calvin, marriage is for opposite sexes and though sex is permissible, temperance is required.[20] Evident in these theologies of marriage is that sexual intercourse is for opposite sexes, and though sex is granted in marriage, it must be limited and limited, as Augustine opines, to the purpose of procreation. No wonder Jordan rightly remarks, sex for Christians is defined by negations.[21]

Christian theology of marriage proposes the biblical idea of "one flesh." While the idea sounds unitive, the problem is that it is reserved only for a heterosexual couple. The unitive function of sex or the concept of "one flesh" is based on the notion of (anatomical) complementarity, where a man, in and through his difference, complements a woman. The notion of complementarity is possible only in heterosexual couplings since the function of the vagina is to receive the penis into itself. Therefore, two men and two women do not fulfil the marital and sexual criterion of complementarity as their physiology restricts such a possibility. This failure leaves them falling short of becoming "one flesh," rendering them inadequate for marital or sexual union. Thus, in traditional Christian theology of marriage, only the marriage between heterosexuals is real marriage, and only sex between heterosexuals is authentic sex. Such a theology upholds heterosexuality, rendering non-heterosexualness as a deficiency.

Even within the Indian contemporary context, "the heterosexuality of marriage is grounded in the procreative imperative."[22] Writing on marriage as a sacrament, George Mathew Kuttiyil states that "sexuality becomes meaningful and complete" only when it is between a man and a woman as that is God's order of creation.[23] Jesudason Baskar Jeyaraj, while believing Christian marriages to be heterosexual with procreation as its end, asserts that a woman's subordination to the man is biblical.[24] Somen Das claims that differentiation of sex in marriage is essential and sex is the sole property of a heterosexual family.[25] In addition, marriages are seen as a remedy for uncontrollable sexuality, as Esther Parajuli reprovingly remarks.[26] These insular values and norms shape and govern family life within Christian communities, and the Church refrains from altering its stance.

Indian marriages are not only gender-biased and sex-biased but also endogamous. There is objection to marrying someone outside a person's local community, clan, tribe or caste. Though there has been the occasional transgression, inter-caste and intercultural marriages are still forbidden amongst most Indian Christian communities for its perceived "polluted" status. The transgressors face abuse and shame, while some are killed in the name of protecting the sanctity of their respective communities. Writing on inter-caste marriage, Samuel Ragland Paul reads caste-based murders as "declarations" by the dominant, where "any threat to the purity of a community will not be tolerated but dealt [with] mercilessly...."[27] The problem within such a culture is that marriage then becomes a social control mechanism that perpetuates communalism and casteism, not to mention its proclivity to hetero/sexism. Marriages that subvert gender roles and community honour do not fit the definition of proper marriage. This is why marriage, for Varghese, is not a biblical ideal at all—it is something the Church does to support society's values.[28] Must not these draconian values be severed?

Reimagining Marriage and Family

While family is generally seen as a system of indoctrination, it is also a subversive social system. In his critique of family values, Jennings interprets Mark 3:21, 31-35 in a way that undermines traditional family ties. Jesus' alternative to the traditional family is clearly evident in the new family, that is a community of believers committed to doing the will of God.[29] The one who does the will of God is the "mother"; not the one who procreates. The blood ties of the old are replaced by the ties of solidarity of the new (this interpretation can even be viewed as a critique of endogamous family and marriage). The ethic that the text seems to project is one that is non-procreative, where emphasis is laid on spiritual procreation as against biological procreation as a means of generating life.[30]

Reflecting on Matthew 10:37—"Whoever loves father and mother more than me is not worthy of me; and whoever loves son or daughter more than me is not worthy of me"—Fritz Wendt says that Jesus envisions "a new social order, an all-encompassing community based on discipleship, rather than biological ties...."[31] Jesus, Wendt observes, makes himself the priority so that family ties and values lose precedence.

This new community, new society, new family is not built on biological connections but on human connections that subvert familial ties.

In Mark 12:18-27, Jesus' response to the Sadducees' question—to which brother would the woman be the wife of?—is worth a mention. In saying that the institution of marriage will not be "resurrected," Jesus denounces the most foundational institution of society.[32] Jennings further points out that what Jesus disqualifies is the future of the institution of marriage and not the erotic or sexuality. Jennings therefore critiques marriage in a way that keeps the sacrament of marriage but erases its "institutionness" and the normalisation of such a sacrament to heterosexuals alone. Though for Jennings, Jesus' new order is a critique of family values and not of sexuality, what has been subtly achieved through such a critique is that sexuality, understood as sex being a procreative act, which is what many understand sexuality to mean and sex to be, is no longer understood as something that prolongs the institution of family. Rather, what propagates familial life is faith; the faith of those who are opposed to the orthodox (and often oppressive) family values and ties. Faith becomes the instrument of *conception* or *origination* and not one's sexuality. In saying this, I do not undermine the role of sexual desire or sexual behaviour in marriage or in any consensual committed relationship. Instead, the point being made is Jesus' emphasis on faith rather than sexuality as the foundation of a family. Or as Ellison contends, "… commitment, not gender and not predetermined roles, is central."[33] Reimagining marriage and family allows for the re/creation of a subversive social system that functions on the principles of justice, love, faith, dependency and equality.

Is Same-sex Relationship a Threat or Promise to Heterosexual Marriage?

Meena Kulkarni, the chief of Mahila Aghadi Samiti, is known to have said, "If women's physical needs get fulfilled through lesbian acts, the institution of marriage will collapse, reproduction of human beings will stop."[34] (Not a bad way to control population escalation, right?) One of the easiest ways to preclude same-sex relationship, apart from appropriating scriptural prohibitions and listing its 'deficiencies,' is to regard it as eroding heterosexual marriage just like Kulkarni did.[35] Rita Nakashima Brock, in her article "Marriage Troubles," engages critically with the normalisation of heterosexual marriage in saying that "heterosexual marriage is biologically, morally and culturally 'normal' or 'natural' because of its procreative purpose."[36] James Brundage's comment is helpful here: "What is natural often means whatever is thought to be the usual practice of the majority." It is obvious from Brock's and Brundage's statements that heterosexual marriage is viewed as being "normal" simply because it is the practice of the majority.

In the debate regarding homosexuality as a threat or promise to marriage and family, one must not conclude that all lesbians and gays are in favour of marriage, even if it incorporated a few alterations. Not everyone advocates marriage. Ashley Tellis, a gay activist in India, finds Indian queer movements' demand for marriage rights elitist. A queer relationship is by default non-heteronormative and marriage is a heterosexual relational model of intimacy, he contends.[37] So for Tellis, marriage is probably the least desirable of ways of living out one's desire and lives.[38] Similarly, for Jewish feminist theologian Judith Plaskow and her partner, marriage contributes to the "perpetuation of a norm of coupledness… [that] marginalizes those who are single, single parents, widowed, divorced, or otherwise living in non-traditional constellations."[39] Echoing what is referenced above, Paula Ettelbrick observes that marriage is the "bearer of the heterosexist norm" deeming illegitimate any form of sexual desire and union that does not align with heteronormativity.[40] Furthermore, critics of marriage suspect that marriage would cause persons to de-emphasise their gayness in order to fit the system. These references highlight how problematic the system of marriage is as it is deeply rooted in heteronormativity and a patriarchal culture. Perhaps, there is much fun and joy when couples live outside the marriage system. Time to… rethink!

If, as noted above, marriage is a heterosexual and patriarchal institution, why do lesbians and gays advocate it? Does it have to do with equal rights? Or, does it go beyond mere rights? While these are pertinent questions demanding answers, I will instead highlight how same-sex relationships can be seen as a promise in its ability to reform the institution of marriage. First, Ellison, for example, says same-sex marriages can teach the Church that sexual orientation is morally neutral.[41] In the same vein, Brock believes that the disruption of gender and power inequalities embedded in heterosexual marriages is something that same-sex relationships can offer.[42] However, this does not mean that same-sex marriages are devoid of patriarchal and hierarchical notions. Third, same-sex relationships can help alter our diminished vision of marriage and family by shifting our focus from a procreative imperative to a *pro-creative* imperative, where creative imaginations of love, family, sex and mutuality take place without restriction and negation. I propose the principle of pro-creativity as it entails the forming and continuing of *life in all its fullness*, not through the act of sexual intercourse but through responsible and creative expressions of one's sexuality towards bodies, feelings, beliefs, and behaviours. The focus shifts from identity to conduct and character of those in relation with each other.[43] This leads me to the fourth promise, where same-sex relationships can restore the unitive function of sex by expanding the expression of sexual desire in diverse forms and practices, thereby negating the primacy and definitiveness of penile-vaginal penetrative sex. If anything, it would make sex more pleasurable.

Marriage and family are not changeless and eternal. They must be altered to *fit the times*. If our theologies of marriage and family remain the same with all its negations and restrictions, communities will continue to be harmed and oppressed. Marriage has been privileged, in legal and religious terms, and this needs to be foiled. Whether legalising same-sex marriage in India will help legislate a change in people's attitudes remains to be seen. But the step towards its legalisation depends on how heterosexuals and a heterosexualised Church begin to think of same-sex relationships. The promises it offers to the institution of marriage are there to see. Some might note that the real problem is the institution of marriage itself and the rest might opine that the real problem is not marriage *per se* but hetero-patriarchal marriage. Whatever position one takes, it is imperative that all work towards undoing heterosexual exclusivism by re-imagining these sociocultural institutions. We would be wise to direct our suspicions against marriage and family than against those who are suspicious of it.

Endnotes

[1] George Weinberg, *Society and the Healthy Homosexual* (New York: St. Martin's Press, 1972), 8.

[2] In the Indian context, it is not wrong to state that homophobia could mean fear in a psychiatric sense. As people tend to have the notion that lesbians and gays could influence, inspire, and "nurture" younger children, fear causes people to disassociate with them.

[3] Robert Goss, *Jesus Acted Up: A Gay and Lesbian Manifesto* (New York: HarperCollins Publishers, 1993), 4.

[4] Judith Butler, *Gender Trouble: Feminism and Subversion of Identity* (New York: Routledge, 2010), 95-97.

[5] Michael Kimmel, "Masculinity as Homophobia: Fear, Shame, and Silence in the Construction of Gender Identity," in *Theorizing Masculinities*, eds. Harry Brod and Michael Kaufman (London/Delhi: SAGE Publications, 1994), 131.

[6] Homosexual anxiety is the "obsessive fear of being or becoming homosexual, the experience of intrusive, unwanted mental images of homosexual behaviour, and/or the obsessive fear that others may believe one is homosexual." See, Monnica Williams, "Homosexuality Anxiety: A Misunderstood Form of OCD," in *Leading-Edge Health Education Issues*, ed. Lennard V. Sebeki (New York: Nova Science Publishers, Inc., 2008), 197.

[7] Gregory M. Herek, "Beyond "Homophobia": Thinking about Sexual Prejudice and Stigma in the Twenty-First Century," *Journal of NSRC: Sexuality Research & Social Policy*, vol. 1, issue 2 (April, 2004): 13.

[8] Romal Laisram, interviewed by the author, Bangalore, March 9, 2017.

[9] Winnie Varghese, *A Journey of Faith: Church and* Homosexuality (Bangalore: BTESSC, 2014), 1. Homophobia, in being a product of social construction, bears the possibility of being deconstructed.

[10] Nivedita Menon, "How Natural is Normal?," in *Because I Have a Voice: Queer Politics in India*, eds. Arvind Narrain and Gautam Bhan (New Delhi: Yoda Press, 2005), 35.

[11] Winnie Varghese, *A Journey of Faith: Church and Homosexuality*, 6. The verse is from Galatians 5:1.

[12] Divya, interviewed by the author, Bangalore, March 4, 2017.

[13] Luke 18:11 (NRSV).

[14] Nick Roen, "Homophobia Has No Place in the Church," *Desiring God*, https://www.desiringgod.org/articles/homophobia-has-no-place-in-the-church (accessed July 14, 2019).

[15] George Zachariah, "Introduction," in *Disruptive Faith, Inclusive Communities: Church and Homophobia*, eds. George Zachariah and Vincent Rajkumar (Bangalore/Delhi: CISRS/ISPCK, 2015), xxvii.

[16] Mark D. Jordan, *The Ethics of Sex* (Malden: Blackwell Publishing, 2002), 117.

[17] Mark D. Jordan, *The Ethics of Sex,* 111-112.

[18] Mark D. Jordan, *The Ethics of Sex,* 115-117.

[19] Mark D. Jordan, *The Ethics of Sex,* 119-120.

[20] Mark D. Jordan, *The Ethics of Sex,* 122.

[21] Mark D. Jordan, *The Ethics of Sex,* 124.

[22] Marvin M. Ellison, *Same-Sex Marriage?: A Christian Ethical Analysis*, (Cleveland: The Pilgrim Press, 2004), 57.

[23] George Mathew Kuttiyil, "Marriage as a Sacrament," in *Christian Family in Transition: Continuity and Discontinuity* (Faridabad: Dharma Jyoti Vidya Peeth, 2012), 22.

[24] Jesudason Baskar Jeyaraj, "Biblical Concept, Imageries and Issues of Marriage," in *Marriage, Family and Church: Holistic Child Development*, vol. 2, ed. by Jesudason Baskar Jeyaraj (Delhi/Bangalore: ISPCK/CFCD, 2014), 6. Jeyaraj presents this hierarchical structure in the name of "participatory governance."

[25] Somen Das, *Christian Ethics and Indian Ethos* (New Delhi: ISPCK, 1994), 17 and 20.

[26] Esther Parajuli, *Sensuous Bodies and Sensuous Texts: Towards a Feminist Theological Understanding of Human Sexuality* (M.Th. (Systematic Theology) Thesis: Senate of Serampore, 2014), 23. In fact in 1 Corinthians 7:9, Paul the celibate tells us that it is better to marry than to live alone burning with passion. What is interesting to note is how marriage is seen as a remedy for uncontrollable sexuality and as a regulator of controlled and limited sexual activity. Ellison notes that marriage is not only founded on sex-negativity but also reinforces it. See, Marvin M. Ellison, *Making Love Just: Sexual Ethics for Perplexing Times* (Minneapolis: Fortress Press, 2012), 69.

²⁷ Samuel Ragland Paul, "God in Dirty Places: Inter-Caste Marriage," *God in Dirty Places,*

https://gindp.blogspot.com/2020/06/day-25-god-in-dirty-places-inter-caste.html (accessed June 12, 2020).

²⁸ Winnie Varghese, *A Journey of Faith: Church and Homosexuality,* 24.

²⁹ Theodore W. Jennings, Jr., *The Man Jesus Loved: Homoerotic Narratives from the New Testament,* (Ohio: The Pilgrim Press, 2003), 175.

³⁰ Theodore W. Jennings, Jr., *The Man Jesus Loved: Homoerotic Narratives from the New Testament,* 216.

³¹ Fritz Wendt, "The Politics of a New 'Family Values'—Matthew 10:24-39," *Political Theology Network,*

https://politicaltheology.com/the-politics-of-a-new-family-values-matthew-1024-39-fritz-wendt/ (accessed June 11, 2020).

³² However, in the Gospel of John, the metaphors of the "bridegroom" and the "wedding feasts" are used positively. See, Theodore W. Jennings, Jr., *The Man Jesus Loved: Homoerotic Narratives from the New Testament,* 195-196, 208.

³³ Marvin M. Ellison, *Same-Sex Marriage?: A Christian Ethical Analysis,* 79. Martha Fineman's proposal is worth noting. She suggests replacing marital family with caretaking family. This shifts the foundation of what a family is built on: from sexual and reproductive affiliation to relationships of dependency and care. See, Martha A. Fineman, *The Autonomy Myth: A Theory of Dependency* (New York: Free Press, 2003), 105-108. Cited in, Marvin M. Ellison, *Same-Sex Marriage?: A Christian Ethical Analysis,* 158.

³⁴ Sunil Mehra, Manu Joseph, and Saira Menezes, "What's Burning?," *Outlook India Magazine,* http://www.outlookindia.com/article. aspx?206676 (accessed June 7, 2020). This comment was made after the release of the 1996 movie *Fire,* a movie depicting love between women.

³⁵ Theodore W. Jennings, Jr., *The Man Jesus Loved: Homoerotic Narratives from the New Testament,* 194.

³⁶ Rita Nakashima Brock, "Marriage Troubles," in *Body and Soul: Rethinking Sexuality in Justice-Love,* eds. Marvin M. Ellison and Sylvia Thorson-Smith (Cleveland: The Pilgrim Press, 2003), 359.

³⁷ "Who's Afraid of Ashley Tellis," *Lavidabibhishikha,*

https://lavidabibhishikha.wordpress.com/2012/10/12/whos-afraid-of-ashley-tellis/ (accessed June 17, 2019).

³⁸ Ashley Tellis, "Should even we live happily ever after?" *DNA,*

https://www.dnaindia.com/analysis/column-should-even-we-live-happily-ever-after-1688029 (accessed June 17, 2019). While Tellis' argument is valid, one must also look at the other side of the coin. Society views marriage and family as the only legitimate space for sexual intimacy and being part of this space accords social acceptance. With this still being the reality in India, lesbians and gays, in need of social acceptance, want to be part of that space. As Ellison and Brock would concede, the answer lies not in the dissolution of marriage but in the reimagining of marriage as a space for intimacy without patriarchal and hierarchical notions.

[39] Marvin M. Ellison, *Making Love Just: Sexual Ethics for Perplexing Times*, 61.

[40] Marvin M. Ellison, *Same-Sex Marriage?: A Christian Ethical Analysis*, 104.

[41] Marvin M. Ellison, *Making Love Just: Sexual Ethics for Perplexing Times*, 64. In saying sexual orientation is morally neutral, Ellison believes that no one gets extra privileges for being heterosexual and no one loses any privilege for being lesbian, gay, bisexual, or a trans person.

[42] Rita Nakashima Brock, "Marriage Troubles," in *Body and Soul: Rethinking Sexuality in Justice-Love*, 359.

[43] Marvin M. Ellison, *Making Love Just: Sexual Ethics for Perplexing Times*, 64.

5

Church and Transgenders[1]

"To put it simply, I feel like a girl trapped in a boy's body, and I've felt that way, ever since I was 4.... When I was 14, I learned what transgender meant, and cried of happiness. After 10 years of confusion, I finally understood who I was. I immediately told my mom, and she reacted extremely negatively, telling me that it was a phase, that I would never truly be a girl, that God doesn't make mistakes, that I am wrong.... The only way I will rest in peace is, if one day transgender people aren't treated the way I was.... My death needs to mean something. My death needs to be counted in the number of transgender people who commit suicide this year. I want someone to look at that number and say let us fix it. Fix society, please fix it." (Leelah) Alcorn

These words from the suicide note written by Leelah Alcorn, who died by suicide on 28 December 2014 in Ohio, USA, raise several pertinent questions. Ministries of *reaching out* to the transgender community offer them care, compassion and support. But Leelah Alcorn's suicide note invites and challenges us to be self-reflective, recognising the role that we, as church and society, continue to play in making them feel that, "The life we live isn't worth living in… because we are transgenders." This calls for an epistemological shift in theological imaginations, and a Damascus experience in faith journeys and mission endeavours. This chapter is an attempt to initiate that process by affirming transgender bodies and lives as theological texts.

Methodological Standpoints

Mission is a term with military connotations. A closer look at colonialism reveals the God-talk that legitimised colonial expansion and subjugation. Mission as conquest was based on three theological convictions: the divinely destined agency of the coloniser to invade and conquer the Other; the teleological vision of an ideal state of maturity, progress and fullness that they wanted to impose upon the colonised with missionary zeal; and a strong sense of deontological call to be the missionaries of this new religion of civilising the Other. We also see the same spirit of mission and conquest in the neoliberal projects of development and globalisation.

Our dominant mission discourses are founded on similar claims. We are convinced of our divine calling to engage in mission. This understanding of mission stems from the presupposition that the beliefs and practices of the "other" are immoral, unnatural and sinful. So, it is our dharma to intervene in the life stories of the "other" and impose our beliefs, practices and moral norms on them and convert them into our understanding of truth and normalcy. Mission has thus become a sacred canopy that legitimises our constructions and representations of the "other," and our interventions in their lives to impose upon them what we consider as the final revelation of truth and morality. Such manifestations of mission are not only accompanied by violence, but are inherently violent.

Over the years, there have been attempts to redeem our missional engagement from this negative legacy of conquest and violence. New paradigms were proposed to widen the horizons of mission to respond to the groaning that emerges from the peripheries of society. However, without a conscious attempt to see beyond the exclusive truth claims and arrogant interventionist strategies, our theological reflections on Christian mission will only contribute to the perpetuation of the prevailing sinful social relations and practices. Said differently, an epistemological break is essential to engage in alternative discourses on mission. In spite of attempts to redeem it, mission continues to be a perspective "from above" legitimising our aggressive interventions in the life of the "other" to forcefully incorporate them into our understanding of normality. External interventions, even if for noble purposes, disable the agency of communities and reduce them to the level of objects to be acted upon.

Such a critical discernment should inspire one to become self-reflective about the missional engagement with the "other," listening to the voices from the margins. According to Mercia McMahon, "The ideal trans theology is the one that is written by the members of the trans communities.... Those who engage in trans positive theology as outsiders need to be careful that they are fully engaging with the community and not making assumptions about what trans people experience…. A trans positive theology should check the interpretations with the trans community and not just source its experiential data there."[2]

Why do we need this epistemological shift? First and foremost, this epistemological shift is the first step to decolonise our theological imagination and missional engagement. Second, it enables the agency of the trans community and transforms them from the state of passive recipients of the benevolence of cisgenders to become subjects of their destiny. Third, it transforms our missional engagement from mission *to* the margins to mission *with* and mission *from* the margins. Fourth, it radically interrogates and disrupts the dominant social constructions of sexuality, family, heteronormativity and gender binaries, and invites us to recognise ourselves as sensual, and sexual beings on a spectrum.[3] As McMahon rightly observes, an "insider prevalence would broaden the subject matter from the seeing phase beyond the standard canon of outsider perspectives."[4] Revathi, an Indian trans activist, shares a similar conviction: "There is no better teacher than lived experience. One should also have empathy and put oneself in the place of another person; see the world from that person's point of view. Unless that happens, we will only be looking at the world through a blinkered vision that sees the world in either black or white. And in doing so we miss the many shades of grey—which is what life is all about."[5] Queer theology is hence used as the methodology in this chapter.

Queer Theology: The Crucible for Developing Trans Theology

The term "queer" literally means to spoil or to interfere with. If the prevailing theological system is already spoiled—spoiled by heteronormativity, homophobia and transphobia—spoiling the spoiled system is the theological imperative to make it more inclusive for people who are already excluded from the body of Christ. Any attempt to define the term "queer" is a rejection of the very meaning of the term. Its non-normative status can be affirmed and celebrated only when we allow the term to remain fluid, multiple and unclear. Nevertheless, we need to clarify the term. For Patrick S. Cheng, the term "queer" can be used in three different ways: *Queer as an Umbrella Term* refers collectively to lesbian, gay, bisexual, transgender, intersex, and all those who do not identify themselves with normative constructions of sexualities and gender identities, yet practice radical solidarity with the queer community. *Queer as Transgressive Action* refers to an ethical standpoint where claims of normativity and false binaries are contested and transgressed. *Queer as Erasing Boundaries* seeks to challenge, disrupt and erase fixed binary categories to affirm sexual and gender fluidity.[6] As Arvind Theodore rightly puts it, "A queer is a person who affirms one's own identity and humanity by rejecting fixed, given, normative categories and the dominant heteronormative culture. If used as a methodological approach, it questions the existence of and disembowels social normative claims, hierarchies, and power relations."[7]

The methodological standpoint of this chapter to place trans theology within the Queer theology movement is intentional and political. In spite of their differences, transgender communities are part of the Queer movement. What binds them together is the experience of marginalisation and violence because of their sexual orientation, gender identity and expression, thanks to dominant religious and societal norms. The transgender community is not homogenous, and they have diverse viewpoints on their relationship with sexual minorities. However, any attempt by outsiders and allies to separate the transgender communities from the larger queer movement and to be in solidarity with them while practising homophobia is unethical and imperialistic.

Towards a Trans Positive Theology

Transgender is an umbrella term used to describe people with a gender identity and expression different to their sex assigned at birth. It may be used to encompass many identities that are outside of a cisgender identity.

Akkai Padmashali is a male-to-female transgender from Bengaluru. She had a confused childhood. She used to wear her sister's dress and play with girls. Her family took her to doctors and traditional healers to cure her. Feeling confused and lonely, at the age of 12 she tried to end her life. As a teenager, Akkai picked up the courage to share her dilemma with other transgender women in a park in Bengaluru. "Don't become like us," they told her. "If you become like us, there are only two options for you—begging or sex work." But Akkai wanted to be like them, and she did. She too had to do sex work for four years. But, interestingly, it is in those years that she came to know that there are many others like her. She never felt lonely any more, and never felt like wanting to die anymore. Seeing the sexual violence that her community faces every day, Akkai was inspired to join a Bengaluru-based NGO that works with sexual minorities. Today, Akkai is the founder-member of Ondede, an organisation that aims to create awareness about sexuality, sexual diversity, and the right to choose one's sexual orientation. Akkai's life is a journey from victim to survivor to thriver. "Being a transgender is not easy. People laugh at you, discriminate against you. You don't have access to buses, public toilets, office spaces. But things are changing now. Why should I die? Let me fight for my community members. I have a huge responsibility on my shoulders."[8]

There are several Akkais in India today, leading the transgender movement and the LGBTIQ movement in different parts of the country. Kerala claims to be a transgender-friendly state. But transphobia continues to manifest in diverse ways in "God's Own Country," and transgenders are harassed, abused, attacked and discriminated against. It is in this context that we initiate this theological and ethical reflections to inspire our faith communities to engage in public witness in solidarity with the transgender communities.

Bible and Christian tradition are ambiguous about Christian discernment and response to ethical issues that we confront in our everyday life. That calls for the mediation of hermeneutics of suspicion and retrieval in our engagement with the sources of our faith. There are several texts in the Bible, popularly known as clobber texts, that legitimise heteronormativity and gender binary. "No one whose testicles are crushed or whose penis is cut off shall be admitted to the assembly of the Lord" (Deuteronomy 23:1). "A woman shall not wear a man's dress, nor shall a man put on a woman's garment; for whoever does such things is abhorrent to the Lord your God" (Deuteronomy 22:5). Both these texts prohibit eunuchs, intersex people, and post-operative transpeople from entering the temple.

We see a similar approach in the policies of churches and Christian organisations. Evangelical Alliance, in its 2001 report, categorically observed that, "Authentic change from a person's given sex is not possible and an ongoing transsexual life is incompatible with God's will." The Vatican also issued a similar statement in 2003: "The key point is that the transsexual surgical operation is so superficial and external that it does not change the personality. If the person was male, he remains male. If she was female, she remains female. The new organs have no reproductive function." What we find in these statements is an attempt to approach ethics as "revealed morality," and to claim exclusive rights to prescribe ethical norms on behalf of God. Further, based on the Natural Law tradition, these statements reject and condemn trans life because: One, self-castration or loss of fertility involved in transsexuality is a violation of natural law; two, the sole purpose of human sexuality is reproduction, and any sexual activity that does not lead to reproduction is unnatural and hence sinful; and three, sex and gender are determined by

God. God does not make any mistakes. Male/female gender binary is God's purpose. There is no in-between-space in God's plan. Sex reassignment surgery is therefore, against God's natural plan and purpose.

A hermeneutical mediation of retrieval, on the other hand, would offer us a different perspective on Christian ethical engagement with transgenders. "For thus says the Lord: To the eunuchs who keep my Sabbaths, who choose the things that please me and hold fast my covenant, I will give, in my house and within my walls, a monument and a name better than the sons and daughters; I will give them an everlasting name that shall not be cut off" (Isaiah 56: 4-5). This messianic vision is a powerful text that privileges transgenders over sons and daughters (cisgenders and straight people). This vision of transgressive messianic politics unveils the queerness of God and God's mission and politics. Queer contests and transgresses the normal, the legitimate, and the dominant. This messianic vision affirms the queer positionality of God.

Trans theology is deeply indebted to Patristic theology and its affirmation of God as mystery. Apophatic theology affirms the unknowability of God. In Apophatic theology the emphasis is on journeying movements and change; not on fixity and perfection. Since we are created in the image of God, our understanding of God is important for us to understand ourselves. Apophatic theology opens up the possibility to reimagine God beyond any single gender identity or sexual expression. God is therefore a *trans*-God. As B.K. Hipsher beautifully narrates, "We need a *trans*-God alright… one that *trans*gresses all our ideas about who and what God is and can be, one that *trans*ports us to new possibilities for how God can incarnate in the multiplicity of human embodiments, one that *trans*figures our mental images from limitations, one that *trans*forms our ideas about our fellow humans and ourselves, one that *trans*cends all we know or think we know about God and about humanity as the *imago Dei*."[9] Hipsher's imagination of God as *trans*-God is transgressive and creative, and it offers us profound insights to liberate God from our notions of heteronormativity and gender binaries. Yes, God is a many gendered reality and experience, and this theological affirmation has profound implications for reimagining who we are as human beings.

Incarnation is God's sending out of love, and for that God had to come out. For Megan More, incarnation is all about the transgendered Christ, understanding and experiencing Christ as the whole expression of all that is human. It was manifested in the birth of Jesus.[10] We also meet the transgendered Christ in the ministry of Jesus. "He broke with every tradition, even in the rejection of all traditional male models of behavior and custom, all in an effort to show that the love of humankind carried more weight than the letter of the law. Jesus even assumed the role of a female and servant. His actions demonstrated breaking with gender normative behavior both in willingly engaging in action or behavior that was strictly for women, and in his rejection of a normal acceptable Jewish male lifestyle."[11] More calls this the queer manifestations of grace!

Lewis Reay's interpretation of Matthew 19 offers us new insights to understand Jesus as the transgendered Christ.

"For there are eunuchs who have been so from birth, and there are eunuchs who have been made eunuchs by others, and there are eunuchs who have made themselves eunuchs for the sake of the kingdom of heaven" (Mathew 19: 12). This is the gospel of inclusivity. Reign of God is where no one is excluded, even the most marginal outsider is included: those who are born intersex, those who are transgender, and those who are gender different, not conforming to normative definitions of gender roles and identities. All those who are marginalised by virtue of their gender expression are part of the community of the reign of God.

Further, by using the term "eunuch" for him and his community, Jesus placed himself permanently out of place, a liminal position. Queer—beyond categorisation, beyond gender binaries. "In entering queer (trans) space, we find normative boundaries blurred, dualistic definitions refuted and the creation of permissive identities. It is in this space that we enter the kingdom of heaven, a world without the confines of traditional, patriarchal structures, systems and roles. Jesus' notion of the reign of God questions identities and blurs distinctions of the normative social categories and social roles of the time."[12] For the trans community, Jesus is their "transcestor"!

Trans theological reimagination and reformulation of the doctrine of God and the doctrine of Christ is not an attempt to engage in metaphysical doctrinal discourses; rather it is an attempt to make sense of their own lives as created in the image of God and redeemed by Christ. Gregory of Nyssa's interpretation of the implications of Apophatic theology for human beings is instructive here. "Let us change in such a way that we may constantly evolve towards what is better, being transformed from glory to glory, and thus always improving and ever becoming more perfect by daily growth, and *never arriving at any limit of perfection.* For perfection consists in our *never stopping in our growth in good, never circumscribing our perfection by any limitation.*"[13] As Susanna Cornwall summarises, "Human gender is important. However, it is not ultimate. Our gender identities are not the final word about us; they are part of our becoming but they are not becoming itself, which is always ahead, always beyond, always delayed. We have, indeed, not reached the limits of our perfection."[14] Said differently, diverse gender expressions and sexual orientations are part of our being and becoming human beings created in the image of God and redeemed by Christ.

Remagining and Reinventing *Ekklesia* as Presence

The history of the institutionalised Church is the history of building walls to exclude and excommunicate communities that transgress the "natural" norms of human life, calling them infidels, sinners, immoral, impure and heretics. The Church is called to become a rainbow community of hospitality, fellowship, and solidarity. The Church has to undergo a radical conversion and become a rainbow community that welcomes the ones who are labelled as immoral and impure and provide them hospitality and fellowship, and struggle with them to create a rainbow world. It requires boldness to queer the understanding and practice of mission. There is a need to go beyond ideas of "feel-good" mission that continues to engage in mission *to* transgenders, where transgenders remain as an empirical category, without names and faces. "Reaching out" to communities as if God is absent in their life stories and history needs to end. Mission from the perspective of trans theology demands at least three responses from the Church: one, to engage in radical interrogation, two, to become intersectional, and three, to participate in queer activism.

Radical interrogation entails the commitment and the courage to interrogate and transgress dominant notions about gender binaries, gender expressions and sexual orientations. Mission, according to trans theology, is not about transpeople *per se*; it is about all of us, and to enable all of us to liberate ourselves from rigid fixities with regard to our gender identity and sexual orientation. As the open letter of the European Orthodox Christian Youth to the Orthodox Church categorically affirms: "Even though LGBT people are quite often presented as being a group external to the Orthodox Church, the proportion of people of non-traditional sexual orientation and gender identity is the same within the Orthodox Church as it is outside. We ask you: in your sermons and speeches, whenever you mention LGBT persons and issues, remember that we actually might be standing right before you! We are not an abstract concept, but actual human beings—your children, sisters, and brothers."[15] Coming out of the closet as a sexual minority requires transgressing the confining expectations that are theologically and ethically justified by the Church. Here the Church is called to accompany sexual minorities in their coming out process. Pastoral care and counselling of transgendered and queer youth and their parents should go beyond curing and correctional techniques and counselling. The society and the Church need to accompany them even as they grapple with the mysteries of their gender and sexuality.

Radical interrogation should also question the way we determine what is good for the transgender community. Looking from the straight privileged position, many people tend to see transgenders as victims who need protection, care, compassion and voice. Radical interrogation should humble the Church into listening to their stories, desires and dreams and reimagining mission as mission *from* and *with* the transgender community. Transgenders are sexual and sensual beings who long for intimacy and relationships. But not only are they disenfranchised sexually, but also are desexualised. Is the mission engagement with transgenders broad enough to fulfil their dreams of being married and to adopt and be parents?

A trans theological understanding of mission affirms *intersectionality*, and requires from the Church the commitment to go beyond the "single-issue" approach. Missional engagements with the transgender community should recognise how multiple forms of oppression contribute to the marginalisation of transpeople. Patriarchy, casteism, ethnicity and class are ideologies and practices of exclusion that transgenders have to confront, along with dominant notions of gender and sexuality. So, mission *with* the transgender communities should link the Church to the struggles of women, Dalits, Adivasis, poor, and queer communities.

Finally, mission *with* transgender communities is a mission of *radical activism*. Mission is public witness, and it requires the nerve to take public stances on critical issues. In the Orthodox understanding of mission, Church is presence. How does the Church become a therapeutic, empowering and transforming presence in the lives of transgenders? If the Church is genuine about its mission *with* transgenders, we need to become a sanctuary for them. If God can accept us *just as we are,* then the Church should become a safe space and sanctuary for transpeople to occupy that space to experience life in its fullness without any conditions. The Church has to incarnate as presence in the streets, where transgender people are harassed and attacked and humiliated. Missional engagement with the transgender community should lead the Church to participate in the ongoing campaigns to repeal regressive laws such as Section 377 of the Indian Penal Code. A trans theological perspective on mission invites the Church to partner with civil society organisations in the campaign to legalise sex work. "Mission as presence" is also a call to transform medical mission facilities into welcoming and safe spaces for the transgender community to get medical care for sex-reassignment surgery. Mission from a trans theological perspective is all about positionality and bold political stances in the public sphere. Practising affirmative action in favour of transgender community in terms of admissions in church-run educational institutions and appointment in church offices and institutions is proclamation of an inclusive gospel.

"It is our call from God not to become a big powerful church, but rather to learn more and more how to be a movement that leads the whole of the church to a new sense of being faithful, not to rules, not to history (tradition), not to theological treatises—but faithful to a very queer-acting God who is always up to something new and daring."[16] As Pope Francis reminds us, "God is not afraid of new things. That is why God is continuously surprising us, opening our hearts and guiding us in unexpected ways." Let us listen to that still small voice from trans lives and trans bodies and reimagine and reinvent our mission.

Endnotes

[1] This chapter is contributed by George Zachariah, Wesley Lecturer in Theological Studies, Trinity Methodist Theological College, Auckland, Aotearoa New Zealand.

[2] Mercia McMahon, "Trans Liberating Feminist and Queer Theologies," in *This is My Body: Hearing the Theology of Transgender Christians*, eds. Christina Beardsley and Michelle O' Brien (London: Longman and Todd, 2016), 61.

[3] "The term gender spectrum is a way of describing gender without conforming to the gender binary. It denotes gender as a continuum that includes male and female, but without establishing them as absolutes or polar opposites. The view of gender as a spectrum allows for the inclusion of identities besides male and female. Specifically, it allows for the inclusion of intersex people, nonbinary gender identities, and nonbinary gender expressions. A person can fall anywhere on the gender spectrum regardless of their orientation, gender expression, or biological sex."

[4] Mercia McMahon, "Trans Liberating Feminist and Queer Theologies," 65.

[5] Revathy, *A Life in Transactivism*, (New Delhi: Zubaan, 2016), xxi.

[6] Patrick S. Cheng, *An Introduction to Queer Theology: Radical Love* (New York: Seabury Books, 2011), 5-8.

[7] Arvind Theodore, "A Christian Ethical Response to Homosexuality with Special Reference to Homophobia in the Indian Christian Community." An Unpublished M.Th. (Christian Ethics) Thesis, The United Theological College, Bengaluru, 2017.

[8] Bhagirath Iyer, "At 12 She Wanted to Die. Today She is Inspiring Hundreds to Fight for Transgender Rights & Justice," *The Better India*,

https://www.thebetterindia.com/21961/how-jagadeesh-became-akkai-padmashali-and-a-transgender-activist-was-born/

[9] B.K. Hipsher, "God is a many Gendered Thing: An Apophatic Journey to Pastoral Diversity," in *Trans/Formations,* eds. Marcella Althaus-Reid and Lisa Isherwood (London: SCM Press, 2009), 97.

[10] With Mary being impregnated by the Holy Spirit, which Christian tradition reflects as feminine, Jesus is born with no male interaction, giving questions to the chromosomal nature of Mary as intersexed, born with a female body but with XY chromosomes enabling her to reproduce without outside male influence. This could also account to Jesus' transgendered nature, since Mary could have been born of a genetic and chromosomal anomaly with elements passed on to her son.

[11] Megan More, "The Transgendered Christ," in *Queering Christianity: Finding a Place at the Table for LGBTQI Christians,* ed., Robert E. Shore-Goss et. al., (Oxford: Praeger, 2013), 95.

[12] Lewis Reay, "Towards a Transgender Theology: Que(e)rying the Eunuchs," in *Trans/Formations,* eds. Marcella Althaus-Reid and Lisa Isherwood (London: SCM Pres, 2009), 157.

[13] Gregory of Nyssa, *On Perfection,* in Danielou 1961, 84.

[14] Susannah Cornwall, "Apophasis and Ambiguity: The Unknowingness of Transgender," in *Trans/Formations,* eds. Marcella Althaus-Reid and Lisa Isherwood, (London: SCM Pres, 2009), 38.

[15] Mary Harris, "LGBT Community Pens Open Letter to the Orthodox Church," *Greek Greece Reporter,*

http://greece.greekreporter.com/2016/06/24/lgbt-community-pens-open-letter-to-the-greek-orthodox-church/

[16] Robert E. Shore-Goss et. al., (ed.), *Queering Christianity: Finding a Place at the Table for LGBTQI Christians,* (Oxford: Praeger, 2013), 48.

6

Interrogating Caste and Masculinity

Masculinity, while being a question of public importance, also becomes a serious theological and ethical problem since dominant understandings of masculinity reinforce and justify the negative treatment of women, men and members of the LGBTQ+ community. Sexuality is never understood and interpreted in a vacuum; hence, this chapter would interrogate the nexus between caste, masculinity, and sexuality. I also attempt to expose how masculinity and caste operate in desexualising sexuality with references to the power imbalances that exist between a Dalit body and a non-Dalit body. In conclusion, I propose the need to Cast(e) rate Masculinity.

Masculinity is derived from the Middle English *masculin* from Middle French and Latin *masculinus* (male) and *masculus* (male).[1] Masculine means having qualities or appearance traditionally associated with men. It has to do with particular traits and qualities rather than with just biology. The equivalents for masculine are male, manlike, manly, bold, brave, macho, muscular, powerful, red-blooded, etc., and this is a reflection of what societies consider a 'real man.' Masculinity is a social definition given to boys and men by societies; it is a social construct.[2] Since masculinity is always constructed in terms of what one is not rather than what one is, Kimmel states that, "[the] notion of anti-femininity lies at the heart of contemporary and historical conceptions of manhood."[3] Patriarchal notions of masculinity are constructed within a heterosexual province and, therefore, we could say that masculinity, in being an expression of gender roles, stands in opposition to femininity through manifestations of control and dominance, even over bodies and sexualities.

Homophobia and Masculinity

Philip Culbertson argues that men grow up viewing intimacy to imply femininity and therefore avoid touching men or being touched by men.[4] Because they are taught that physical touch is sexually loaded, men fear being intimate with men in just about any form. This connotes that there is a connection between patriarchy, masculinity and homophobia. In wanting to highlight the interconnection between masculinity and homophobia, I turn to James Nelson who offers five reasons why heterosexual men are repelled by gays.[5] First, homophobia is predominant in heterosexual men as homoeroticism is projected to be disgusting by societies. Second, since gays are stereotyped as being sexually active, heterosexual men perceive them as being more 'male' than themselves; this causes rage and envy. Third, gays sabotage patriarchy as they take on the receptive function, i.e., embodying the symbol of a 'woman.' Fourth, the fear of heterosexual men being treated as sexual objects by gays just the way heterosexuals objectify women is appalling. And finally, gays seeking validation, love, and affection from other men is frightening for heterosexual men.

The above reasons suggest how a heteronormative understanding of masculinity and its functioning can have a detrimental impact on one's perception of and relationship with gay men. Patriarchy, as noted in chapter four, needs heterosexuality for its survival and heterosexuality needs homophobia for its ascendency over other forms of sexual preference. Homophobia becomes a weapon of heterosexism and male chauvinism when homophobia, having its roots in heterosexism, is enforced by patriarchy.

What is evident in Nelson's reasoning is that heterosexual men have an aversion towards gay men and feel threatened by them as the latter "emasculates" and "unmans" the former.[6] Kimmel notes, "Homophobia is the central organizing principle of our cultural definition of manhood."[7] While, he says this in his North American context, it is no different from ours. Interestingly, heterosexual men espouse homophobia as lesbians become insurgents in a male-chauvinistic society threatening their masculinity by going against the norm in rejecting men as the only competent ones able to complete or consummate their personhood.[8] Now take a moment to dwell on that! While almost all societies are patriarchal in some way or the other, in India the potency of patriarchy is almost inestimable. Varghese, therefore, speaks of the "perverted sexuality of power over" where men dominate women (and gay men as well).[9] A patriarchal society that shelters hegemonic forms of masculinity is ripe ground for homophobia to flourish.

Masculinism and Sexual Relations

This virulent notion of masculinity has pervaded heterosexual relationships, and quite problematically crept into gay sexual relationships as well. As Tellis points out, the "tops" force the "bottoms" to submit to their sexual desires.[10] The latter are seen as mere objects just the way women are viewed. Tellis is warning against idealising sexual relations between men as the influence of patriarchal and masculinist displays of power and control are not absent.[11] If anything, both feminism and masculinity studies have taught us to perceive the phallus as the locus of men's power, thereby making even the *erotic* as potential locations of power imbalances.[12] While I am not suggesting that receptivity be viewed as passivity or subservience, one cannot evade the gratification experienced in playing the dominant or masculine role. I am careful not to moralise the functioning of different roles played, but rather stating the mechanics of penetrative-receptive sexual acts.

Established socioeconomic systems reify the masculinity-sexuality nexus to the extent that social and economic imbalances can determine the individual's position and function in a sexual act. The top-bottom dynamic is not the property of heterosexual relations alone (though I must concede that the logic is based on a heteronormative understanding of sexual relations). Emphasis on the receptive partner's demonstration of "body-rooted authority," as Goh puts it while describing and analysing the 'receptive' experience of a gay man, could preclude one from perceiving and problematising the exertion of power by the *active* partner.[13] Also, forms of social privilege such as sex, ethnicity, caste and class that shape one's narratives and body-mediated experiences cannot be ignored. A critical analysis of the functioning of such dynamics in non-heterosexual arrangements must take place, but it can happen only upon the recognition of the danger that a heteronormative framework poses in understanding sexual relations.

Masculinity in the Indian Context

Since masculinity is socially constructed and each society differs from one another, one must avoid homogenising masculinity. So it only makes sense to make a brief reference to Indian masculinity or masculinity in the Indian context keeping in mind the following section that interrogates the power imbalances that exist between a Dalit body and a non-Dalit body. When one speaks of Indian masculinity, it is generally interpreted in the line of Hindu masculinity and colonial masculinity. Chandrima Chakraborty states that imperial masculinity was normative during the British rule in India, as Indian masculinity was viewed as effeminate. Most Indians were considered unfit to be part of the government due to their "biological make-up and sociohistorical conditioning," she observes.[14] While Chakraborty delineates the history of colonial masculinity,[15] Kajri Jain traces how the Hindu depiction of "Divine Muscularity" influenced Indian masculinity and vice versa.[16] Though muscularity was not a prominent feature in Indian masculinity, it began to be shaped by religion, culture, class, caste, geography, globalisation and capitalism.[17] Even nationalism was highly influenced by a type of masculinity that was idealised by

Mohandas Karamchand Gandhi.[18] That said, what we see today is remasculinisation through violence against minorities, such as Muslims and Dalits. This is viewed as a cure for the alleged crisis in Hindu masculinity, assuming it to have the potential to wipe away centuries of subjugation inflicted by the colonisers. Hindutva projects violence as "natural" and propagates the idea of the "angry" Hindu. Its ideology is to transform a "weak" and "emasculated" masculinity into men with the capital 'M.'[19] This clearly highlights how masculinity, in embodying violence and aggression, becomes a strategy of achieving and maintaining participation and domination in the environments in which men live.

The Dalit Body

In order to explore the nexus between caste and masculinity more deeply, I shall begin this section by making a brief reference to the caste system and a reference to Dalits and the narratives surrounding the construction of a Dalit body. Caste, or *varna*—a term used to denote caste—refers to the fourfold division of society based on *function*. It is believed that Hindu scriptures, i.e., the *Vedas*, divided and divinised the division of society into *varnas* in the post-Vedic period. The four *varnas* are *Brahman* (priest), *Kshatriya* (warrior), *Vaishya* (trader), and *Shudra* (servant).[20] Dalits are those who fall outside the fourfold *varna* system.[21] Since they do not form a part of the body of Brahma from which the four *varnas* originate, they have historically been called "untouchables" and "outcaste" for their perceived 'impurity.'

The concept of purity and pollution functions as the foundational principle of the caste system. Writing on Dalit bodies as "Bodies that don't matter," (perhaps taking a cue from Butler's "Bodies that Matter"), Joshua Samuel states that "caste operates through the negation of the other" and is sustained by the reification of untouchability fuelled by notions of purity and pollution[22] (notice how caste, as Samuel notes, and masculinity, as Kimmel points out, are defined by the negation of the other and by what they are not). While this points to the nexus between the concept of purity and pollution and the caste system, it is also important to note how the concept functions within the logic of boundary maintenance. Because Dalits are considered to be inherently "polluted," there are strict social markers that they ought not to cross. For the social order and caste system to exist, the difference between "within and without, above and below… with and against…" must be exaggerated and maintained.[23] Any transgression of social boundaries is quickly countered with violence. Conversely, violence is used to prevent any transgression of social boundaries.

Sundar John Boopalan understands that some bodies are habituated to exercising control over other bodies and in doing so force the 'inferior' bodies to assume positions of servitude.[24] In order for Dalit bodies to assume positions of servitude they need to be watched, disciplined, and controlled, and to ensure the disciplining and monitoring of Dalit bodies, dominant-caste bodies use violence. But, as Michel Foucault in his book *Discipline and Punish* states, disciplining need not always involve the use of violence. He says that disciplining "may be calculated, organised, technically thought out; it may be subtle, make use of neither weapons nor of terror and yet remain of a physical order."[25] What is significant here is not just violence enacted on Dalit bodies, but also the threat of violence. In this 'violent' pattern of interactions between bodies, the Dalit body becomes the disciplined body and the dominant-caste body becomes the disciplining body. What I intend to convey is that caste accords power to individuals, which in turn allows them to control, monitor, and discipline other bodies—be it that of women, transpersons, gays, lesbians, bisexuals, intersexed persons or queers. Power derived through caste is violent and savage.

The Caste-Sexuality-Masculinity Nexus

All people are generally conditioned into societies as gendered beings through a complex web of obligations, expectations, and social relations. They are expected to behave according to their orientations with respect to caste, class, race and region as power is accompanied with the same. Hence, power inherited by people in belonging to certain castes is exercised on Dalit bodies to control and define expectations and roles. This power not only decides the physical boundaries but also monitors the desires, experiences, and expressions of the body. Writing on masculinity, Kimmel opines that a show of any hint of powerlessness from the dominant is nothing less than a fall from grace.[26] In applying the same logic to caste supremacy, one can argue that a dominant-caste person's failure to exercise power over the "Other" is considered to be a sign of weakness. Because a dominant-caste person inherits from their caste affiliations the power and command to control other bodies, an 'impure' Dalit body poses a problem and a threat to the dominant-caste body. Overt violence is accompanied by subtle forms of violence exercised by controlling the social movement and the economics of a Dalit body. As Boopalan observes, "Cycles of violence are often cycles of habituated behavior in which certain human bodies are moving in modes that discriminate, exclude, and render some bodies inferior to others."[27] Following this line of reasoning, caste violence is to be understood as a manifestation of power, power over Dalit bodies.

At the heart of hegemonic masculinity—a form of masculinity that contains sexist and misogynistic tenets allowing men to maintain their patriarchal privilege over women—lies the notion of anti-femininity.[28]. Writing on the nexus between caste and masculinity, Kalpana and Vasanth Kannabiran state that, "... 'manhood' of the caste is defined both by the degree of control men exercise over women and the degree of passivity of the women of the caste."[29] Likewise, violently disciplining the female Dalit body is, according to Clarke, "a tactic used by caste communities to demonstrate the power they have over all Dalit life."[30] When dominant-caste men abuse Dalit bodies they re-establish the idea that Dalit women have no 'purity' and 'honour.' The casteism-sexism mode of disciplining the body becomes a deadly form of violence. Assaults on Dalit women not only speaks to the female Dalit body but to the male Dalit body as well, highlighting the latter's incapability of 'protecting' the former.[31] If male Dalit bodies are mocked for its inability to protect the female Dalit body, the gay male Dalit body is loathed for assuming the role and function of a female body. This further translates to the hatred and loathing of queer bodies, especially gay men and transwomen. In the process of 'othering the Other'—the female Dalit body and queer Dalit bodies—the heterosexual male non-/Dalit body constructs a pure self.[32] Therefore, one can notice in raping, lynching, and murdering of Dalits the motive to discipline the Dalit body.

As mentioned earlier, one cannot speak of sexuality in India without juxtaposing it with caste. Speaking of the sexuality-caste nexus, Jayachitra states how sex, sexuality and sexual expressions are regulated by the caste system. In the *Manusmriti*, if a twice-born male (*dvija*) commits an offence that is unnatural with another man, the person has to undertake purity rituals.[33] However, she notes that the term *Dvija* refers to Brahmins alone,[34] indicating how only they could practice these sexual ideals, which further implies that the sexual desires of the dominant-caste men were superior to those belonging to oppressed communities.[35] While the *Kamasutra*, as we know, epitomised sexual variations, it was patronised only by caste elites and that with women and transgenders of the 'lower-caste.'[36] Even though oral sex was permissible between homosexuals according to the *Kamasutra*, certain *Dharmashastras*, Ruth Vanita states, project oral-genital contact permissible only within heterosexual relations and not within homosexual relations.[37] From the above findings and statements, one can deduce two things: one, that sexual variations including the practice of same-sex desire was coloured by caste; and two, that only dominant-caste men could afford to experiment with their sexualities and manhood.

Cast(e)rating Masculinity

As men acquire power and access to bodies through their caste affiliations, I propose the idea of cast(e)rating masculinity. To cast(e)rate masculinity is to have men cast(e)rate themselves from the power and license to act on the power that caste concedes. It is vital that men strip themselves of that power, a sign of undoing caste or men 'unmanning' caste. To cast(e) rate hegemonic masculinity is to hope men would undo their dominant caste affiliations for the good of humanity, which would leave them free of the oppressive power that binds their being. This in turn would allow men to embrace their vulnerability—something they have been conditioned to conceal. Vulnerability is often seen as a weakness, so men avoid it. But as Rochhuathanga Jongte observes, "… vulnerability serves as a critique to the dominant masculinity..."[38] If men embrace vulnerability, signs of toughness and dominance would be replaced by a desire for bonding and expressions of emotional intimacy. Embracing one's vulnerability opens up avenues for relationality and change that in turn would leave men risking their 'manhood' for the sake of human goodness.

Cast(e)rating hegemonic masculinity would further allow men to embrace femininity and other masculinities. It would also help deconstruct themselves, disassociate themselves from homophobia, queerphobia, misogyny, and casteism, and put on a more gentle and inclusive construction. Cast(e)rating masculinity involves the renunciation of possessions such as "the possession of power over the Other, the possession of 'rights' over the Other, the possession of privilege before the Other."[39] It entails abandoning the need to acquire a manhood patterned after patriarchal ideologies, calling for a dogged refusal to use abusive power that caste and maleness accord. Since the caste-masculinity nexus legitimises violence against women, men and queer subjects, it is important for (heterosexual) men, as Dalit theologian Joseph Prabhakar Dayam urges, to interrogate and audit their gendered self and come to an awareness of being located in a position of power.[40] He rightly insists that men must question the influences that shape their being, the perspectives they hold as men, and the actions they perform.[41] Only when men come to an awareness of being located in a position of power can they distance themselves from the abusive power that caste accords. In sum, to cast(e)rate masculinity is to scrutinise, identify and distance oneself from hegemonic displays of masculinity; undo dominant teachings and interpretations of sexuality and gender that valorise men; challenge the male-chauvinistic patriarchal political, economic and social settings; and create communities of solidarity where all femininities and masculinities can be welcomed, affirmed and celebrated.

The masculine culture we live in continues to reinforce the notion of masculinity by valorising macho, muscular, red-blooded men. Remember the old advertisements that promulgated messages such as *"men are back"* (Maruti Suzuki SX4) or *"definitely male"* (Bajaj Pulsar) that suggest how a 'real man' ought to be? These images have conditioned and continue to condition our minds. When hegemonic masculinity is elevated, images of femininity and other masculinities are marginalised and subordinated. Does this not determine our perception of femininity and masculinity? Our reluctance in dealing with such issues has a considerable bearing on the injustices in our societies. Men must therefore challenge themselves to examine their masculine vices that have perpetuated evil in public and in private forums. Masculinity in itself is not flawed, but when men wield masculine (and homophobic) displays of power, dominance, violence, hatred and aggression, it becomes hegemonic and life-negating, and that needs to be critiqued and changed. Every person is created in the image of God the Creator, and this image cannot be celebrated in isolation but only in togetherness and in partnership. Cast(e)rating masculinity allows for the possibilities for such a celebration.

Endnotes

[1] Jeff Hearn "Masculinity/Masculinities," in *International Encyclopedia of Men and Masculinities,* ed. Michael Flood, et al. (London: Routledge, 2007), 390.

[2] Kamala Bhasin, *Exploring Masculinity* (New Delhi: Women Unlimited, 2004), 5-6.

[3] Michael Kimmel, "Masculinity as Homophobia: Fear, Shame, and Silence in the Construction of Gender Identity," in *Theorizing Masculinities,* eds. Harry Brod and Michael Kaufman (London/Delhi: SAGE Publications, 1994), 126. Kimmel defines hegemonic masculinity as an image of masculinity of those men who hold power, and this power is destructive power as it grants men the power to control women and other men.

[4] Philip Culbertson, "Explaining Men," in *Sexuality and the Sacred: Sources for Theological Reflection*, eds. James B. Nelson and Sandra P. Longfellow (Kentucky: Westminster/John Knox Press, 1994), 190.

[5] James B. Nelson, *The Intimate Connection: Male Sexuality, Masculine Spirituality* (London: SPCK, 1992), 61-62.

[6] The "domination" by a penis whether literally or figuratively is obnoxious to the heterosexual mind. Because the penetrated male "lacks" the power to penetrate, he symbolizes unmanliness, posing a threat men's masculinity. See, Miguel A. De La Torre, *A Lily among the Thorns: Imagining a New Christian Sexuality,* 155.

[7] Michael Kimmel, "Masculinity as Homophobia: Fear, Shame, and Silence in the Construction of Gender Identity," 131.

[8] James B. Nelson, *Body Theology* (Kentucky: Westminster/John Knox Press, 1992), 68.

[9] Winnie Varghese, "Eliminating Homophobia in the Indian Church: The Goodness of the Body," in *Disruptive Faith, Inclusive Communities: Church and Homophobia*, 229.

[10] Ashley Tellis, "The bad sex award goes to gay Indian men," *DNA*
https://www.dnaindia.com/lifestyle/report-the-bad-sex-award-goes-to-gay-indian-men-1749720 (accessed June 9, 2020).

[11] I must add that not all gays engage in penetrative sex. The issue is not with the act of penetration but rather the heteronormative ideologies that guide sexual relationships and acts.

[12] While the phallus is seen as a symbol of power, aggression, and control, there are communities like the Hispanics, for whom the "signifier of signifiers" are the *cojones* (testicles) and not the penis. Miguel A. De La Torre, *Liberating Sexuality: Justice Between the Sheets* (Saint Louis: Chalice Press, 2016), 120.

[13] Joseph N. Goh, *Living Out Sexuality and Faith: Body Admissions of Malaysian Gay and Bisexual Men*, 72. For a deeper analysis of the sexual acts of gay men, consider reading the chapter "Sexplorations."

[14] Chandrima Chakraborty, *Masculinity, Asceticism, Hinduism: Past and Present Imaginings of India* (Ranikhet: Permanent Black, 2011), 22.

[15] There were few models of masculinity that the Indian men considered emulating: the Aryan model of aggressive kshatriyahood; the self-denying ascetic brahmanhood; and the model that was associated with the bhakti movements (androgyny). Indians, out of lack of "self-esteem" and forgotten "manhood," had to emulate some form of masculinity and so, seeing the British as agents of change and modernisation, adopted the imperialistic masculinity that was aggressive in nature. While some adopted the masculinity proposed by kshatriyahood, some others embraced the ascetic manhood. The problem, however, with the ascetic model was that though manhood was not evident in the physical structure of the person, it began to reflect the dominant caste male Hindu masculinity and marginalised the rest. It generated communitarianism and casteism. See, Chandrima Chakraborty, *Masculinity, Asceticism, Hinduism: Past and Present Imaginings of India*, 23-24.

[16] For certain deities, the source of strength does not lie in the physical attributes but in a transcendent power. Certain images of Ram do not show muscularity. However, Hanuman is often depicted having muscular strength.

Such a body casts a certain value to muscular agency. Similarly, in some images, one can notice a muscular Krishna. Jain further goes on to state that the transition from Ram being portrayed without muscularity in the later years appears in contrasting images. Her argument is that while in some ways the divine muscularity/masculinity influenced human muscularity/ masculinity, human muscularity/masculinity (particularly from the cinema field) began to influence divine muscularity/ masculinity. See, Kajri Jain, "Muscularity and its Ramifications: Mimetic Male Bodies in Indian Mass Culture," in *Sexual Sites, Seminal Attitudes: Sexualities, Masculinities and Culture in South Asia,* ed. Sanjay Srivastava (New Delhi: SAGE Publications, 2004), 308-328.

[17] Sanjay Srivastava, "Non-Gandhian Sexuality, Commodity Cultures and a 'Happy Married Life': Masculine and Sexual Cultures in the Metropolis," in *Sexual Sites, Seminal Attitudes: Sexualities, Masculinities and Culture in South Asia,* 365.

[18] Non-violence, vegetarianism, and sexual abstinence was Gandhi's form of masculinity. By projecting brahmacharya as central to the performance of political and ethical duties, Gandhi privileged the male discourse on sexuality. While some saw positive functionability in this, it submerged femininity. For Gandhi, (Hindu) women's ability to endure suffering was the highest form of ahimsa. A selfless, loving mother and a desexualised widow were Gandhi's feminine ideals. This understanding of masculinity and femininity in many ways reformed the body politic allowing Gandhi to embark on his national programme. See, Chandrima Chakraborty, *Masculinity, Asceticism, Hinduism: Past and Present Imaginings of India,* 133-134.

[19] Chandrima Chakraborty, *Masculinity, Asceticism, Hinduism: Past and Present Imaginings of India,* 176-191.

[20] Peniel Rajkumar, *Dalit Theology and Dalit Liberation: Problems, Paradigms and Possibilities* (Surrey: Ashgate Publishing Limited, 2010), 4. The word *Dalit* has its roots in the Sanskrit word *Dal,* meaning broken, oppressed, and the Hebrew root word *Dal,* meaning weak, frail, humiliated, oppressed. It must also be mentioned that the term "Dalit" was chosen by Dalits themselves and therefore they use the term to affirm their dignity and worth. Debjani Ganguly notes the term's political underpinnings as "anti-Brahmanical, anti-upper caste, anti-patriarchal" can be traced back to Jyotiba Phule, a social reformer. See, Debjani Ganguly, *Caste, Colonialism and Counter-Modernity: Notes on a Postcolonial Hermeneutics of Caste* (London: Routledge, 2005), x. Likewise, Sathianathan Clarke observes that the term is not a caste identity but "an anti-caste collective movement" purposed to dismantle the caste system. See, Sathianathan Clarke, "Dalits Overcoming

Violation and Violence: A Contest between Overpowering and Empowering Identities in Changing India," *The Ecumenical Review*, 54:3 (2002): 279.

[21] Those within the caste system are called *varnas* and those outside of it, the Dalits, are called *avarnas*.

[22] Joshua Samuel, "Untouchable Bodies and Divine Possessions: A Comparative Theology of Liberation" (PhD dissertation, Union Theological Seminary, 2017), 72.

[23] Mary Douglas, *Purity and Danger: An Analysis of the Concepts of Pollution and Taboo* (London/New York: Routledge and Kegan Paul, 1966), 4. Cited in, Peniel Rajkumar, *Dalit Theology and Dalit Liberation: Problems, Paradigms and Possibilities* (Surrey: Ashgate Publishing Limited, 2010), 7.

[24] Sundar John Boopalan, *Memory, Grief and Agency: A Political Theological Account of Wrongs and Rites* (London: Palgrave Macmillan, 2017), 86.

[25] Michel Foucault, *Discipline and Punish: The Birth of the Prison*, second ed., trans. Alan Sheridan (New York: Vintage Books, 1995), 26.

[26] Michael S. Kimmel, *The Gender of Desire. Essays on Male Sexuality* (Albany: State University of New York Press, 2005), 236.

[27] Sundar John Boopalan, *Memory, Grief and Agency*, 75.

[28] Eric Anderson, *Inclusive Masculinity: The Changing Nature of Masculinities* (London: Routledge, 2009), 36.

[29] By the same argument, they state that demonstrating control by humiliating women of other caste is another way of reducing the 'manhood' of those castes. Therefore, sexual assaults on women of oppressed communities are double-edged. When men of dominant caste display hegemonic traits, they not only pass on the message of power relations to the women but also to their men. See, Kalpana Kannabiran and Vasanth Kannabiran, *De-Eroticizing Assault. Essays on Modesty, Honour and* Power (Calcutta: STREE, 2002), 60.

[30] Sathianathan Clarke, "Dalits Overcoming Violation and Violence: A Contest between Overpowering and Empowering Identities in Changing India," *The Ecumenical Review*, 54:3 (2002): 284.

[31] Even as I state that violence exacted on female Dalit bodies by male non-Dalit bodies speak to male Dalit bodies, male Dalit bodies are not innocent. While dominant caste men have sought to control male Dalit bodies either directly or indirectly, Dalit men also seek to control the bodies of Dalit women. The underlying ideology here is that of patriarchy and masculinism and that needs to be unequivocally challenged. In referencing to sexual assaults on Dalit women, I cannot avoid referring to the phallus (the male sex organ in its aroused state)—understood as the symbol

of manliness and the locus of men's power. Since domination or male authority (in rape) is viewed as an erotic category for men and the 'erotic' being invariably defined in terms of masculine power and aggression, one must perceive rape as a form of oppression that legitimises the male as the libertine and the phallus as the epitome of sexual weaponry. Therefore, rape helps men assert their manliness, power, and sexual prowess. If the phallus is viewed as a sexual weapon one need not doubt how masculinity uses rape to endorse and sustain sexual hierarchies. To understand domination as an erotic category, see Deborah L Madsen, *Feminist Theory and Literary Practice* (London: Pluto Press, 2000), 154-155.

[32] Evangeline Anderson-Rajkumar, "Turning Bodies Inside Out: Contours of Womanist Theology," in *Dalit Theology in the Twenty-first Century*, Sathianathan Clarke et.al (New Delhi: Oxford University Press, 2010), 208.

[33] Jayachitra L., "Dalit Theology as Anti-Caste Theology: Musings from Intersexual Dialogue in the Reign of God," in *Disruptive Faith, Inclusive Communities: Church and Homophobia*, eds. George Zachariah and Vincent Rajkumar (Bangalore/Delhi: CISRS/ISPCK, 2015), 166-168.

[34] Though the term earlier denoted the privileged position of men from *Brahmin*, *Kshatriya*, and *Vaishya* caste groups, it later became an exclusive term for *Brahmins*.

[35] Ruth Vanita states that male servants performed oral sex on their masters. While it may suggest that homosexual acts were practised, there is clear evidence of the existence and functioning of social hierarchical mores. Ruth Vanita, "Introduction: Ancient Indian Materials," in *Same-Sex Love in India: A Literary History*, eds. Ruth Vanita and Saleem Kidwai (Haryana: Penguin Random House India Pvt. Ltd., 2008), 32.

[36] That being said, it is interesting and important to note that the 1911 (reprinted in 1934 and in 1995) standard Hindi translation of the *Kamasutra* by Madhavacharya states that oral sex, anal sex, and homosexual activities are wrong forms of sex with the latter being the worst of the lot. While all forms of lovemaking are mentioned in the *Kamasutra*, some are judged to be "base." The author of *Kamasutra* states that everything should be described but not everything is recommended. See, Vatsyayana Mallanaga, *Kamasutra*, trans. and eds. Wendy Doniger and Sudhir Kakar (New York: Oxford University Press, 2002), xx-xxi. Cited in, Margaret A. Farley, *Just Love: A Framework for Christian Sexual Ethics*, (London: Continuum International Publishing Group, 2006), 94.

[37] Ruth Vanita, "Vatsyayana's *Kamasutra*," in *Same-Sex Love in India: A Literary History*, 62.

[38] Rochhuathanga Jongte, *"Imagining Redemptive Masculinity: Towards a Tribal Theological Anthropology* (M.Th. (Systematic Theology) Thesis: Senate of Serampore, 2014), 89.

[39] Miguel A. De La Torre, *Liberating Sexuality*, 35.

[40] Joseph Prabhakar Dayam, "Towards a Liberatory Christian Theology for Men: Interrogating the Gendered Self," in *Created in God's Image: From Hegemony to Partnership*, eds. Patricia Sheerattan-Bisnauth and Philip Vinod Peacock (Switzerland: WCC, 2010), 34.

[41] Joseph Prabhakar Dayam, "Towards a Liberatory Christian Theology for Men: Interrogating the Gendered Self," 34.

7

Reimagining Church as a Sexual Community

Church as a sexual community? Am I stretching my imagination a bit too far? How can one even conceive of sexualising the Church, the holy institution? Indeed, reimagining the Church as a sexual community might sound outrageous or blasphemous to many, but remember the Church is made up of people not buildings, and all people are sexual beings. So whether one likes it or not, agrees or not, the Church has always been a sexual community (but, of course, with many distortions!). However, the task ahead is to repentantly rethink, prophetically reimagine, creatively reorder, and imaginatively revision this sexual community.

The Church has contributed much to sexual injustice and owes much to its elimination. In misunderstanding and misrepresenting the body, the Church has desexed sex, and regrettably continues to remain heterosexist. Back in June 2016, speaking to a few reporters, Pope Francis said that the Church must seek forgiveness from the LGBTQ+ community for having treated them with disdain throughout history. The Pope was found saying,

> "I think that the Church not only should apologize … to a gay person whom it offended but we must also apologize to the poor, to women who have been exploited, to children forced into labor… The question is: if a person who has that condition, who has good will, and who looks for God, who are we to judge?"[1]

This is a powerful statement considering the ecclesial tradition of which the Pope is a part. Many Catholics, Protestants and Free/Pentecostal/Independent Churches in India did not respond kindly to this and made derogatory remarks against the Pope. By negating the validity of the Pope's statement, the Church overtly endorsed homophobia as a religious duty. This, to me, is an insidious menace. Can the Church ever come to recognise its own shortcomings? While it may take longer than desired, I am certain it can. It must.

This chapter would stress the path the Church should take in order to become a community that can accommodate diverse identities and sexualities. Unless the Church revises its ethical sensibilities, it cannot hope to eliminate sexual injustice and view sexuality as viable, legitimate and part of God's good plan.

Why an Inclusive Church is Not Enough

The institutional Church is far from a safe abode. It almost seems like its spirituality has nothing to do with those who suffer. Being obsessed with the idea of "institutionalisation," it systematically alienates and excludes people who do not conform to its ideologies, theologies and practices. To counter this exclusivism, the idea of an inclusive Church was proposed. The concept of inclusivity, proposed by liberation theologians and pastors, became popular during the 1990s.[2] Today, pastors, theologians, and activists continue to envision an inclusive Church.

While the idea of inclusivity seems fascinating, intelligible and necessary, it is not devoid of problems. There are five potential problems I see with the concept of inclusivity. First, the concept epitomises triumphalism. When the Church begins to open its doors to members of the LGBTQ+ community, there is the possibility of self-righteousness and moral superiority creeping into the Church. Becoming inclusive might feel like a moral victory, forgetting the fact that to embrace the 'Other' *is* the ontological characteristic of the body of Christ.[3]

Second, while speaking of an inclusive Church, one must question if members of the community want to be part of a structure that has violated them all along. One cannot assume that the moment the Church claims to be inclusive, people would burst into its space seeking assurance and affirmation. The queer community has always been suspicious of the Church and will continue to be so. The Church must deal with it. On the same issue, Laisram states that queers like him can survive without the Church though he does acknowledge that there are queers who need its fellowship.[4] The Church can open its arms and be welcoming but if queer friends do not feel safe, it would amount to nothing. An embrace becomes an embrace only when it is counter-embraced.

The third problem, and closely related to the second, is that inclusivity is understood in terms of including the other into one's space. This is a shallow interpretation as inclusivity importantly involves the willingness to *be* included. Rather than having queer communities come into its walls, the Church must be willing to go into queer spaces, if and when invited, and be ready to go to public spaces when needed. Inclusivity, here, entails two things: one, it requires political activism; two, it necessitates embracing hospitality. First, political activism is a faith task. The Church has the duty to be publicly critical of the role law, politics and culture play in defining queer people and relegating certain expressions of sexuality to the base. To be inclusive is to be politically conscious. Second, inclusivity necessitates embracing or receiving hospitality from the other. Rather than hoping to affect members of the community through its "mission," the Church must open up itself to be touched, impacted and nourished by them. Only when the Church risks itself for love's sake can it truly become inclusive.

Fourth, the concept of inclusivity functions within a heteronormative framework making heterosexuals the agents of transformation. Here, heterosexuals become the point of reference, making themselves the norm, stealthily desiring to be imitated. Operating under this ideology would make the Church act on the normative impulse to 'reach out' as if having them conform to existing normative patterns of relational modes will make their lives any better. This idea of inclusivity erases the agency of queer people and "their right to be the subjects of their own life."[5] It is perhaps for this reason that the Church must embark on a self-reflective process to first confess its own sins of venerating inequality and sexual hierarchy and disseminating heteronormative patterns of living, reasoning and loving.

Fifth, as Frederico Pieper Pires points out, inclusivity functions with a Hegelian framework. Pires, in pointing out the interconnectedness between Hegel's philosophy of the Absolute Spirit and the concept of inclusivity, argues that both have the intention of homogenising. Here, differences are negated, and if differences are accepted it is done so as to include the other into a heterosexist, phallocentric and hierarchical system.[6] In doing this, inclusivity grants will to the system, erases difference and succeeds in creating, in Hegelian language, a whole.

These concerns must push us to re-think and re-define inclusivity. While the intention to be an all-inclusive Church is appreciable, the consequences that entail, if unchecked, are rather perilous. If inclusivity, on the surface, is not the answer, what alternative paradigm can one seek? How about envisioning a "Repentant Church?"

How about a Repentant Church?

The Church aims at drawing others to repentance so it can exercise the "divinely ordered right" of forgiveness. But my question is, what makes forgiveness the sole property of the Church? If the duty of the Church is to forgive others, is the Church sinless? No, for history reveals how iniquitous the Church has been to women and queers. Divya contends that the Church has been disappointing as it fails to meet LGBTQ+ communities where they are and intends on meeting them only in terms of where they ought to be.[7] The Church in explicitly and pretentiously flaunting moral superiority sins against the queers. This leaves the Church with no option but to repent for its historical and present sins and seek forgiveness from those it has violated. It must repent and humbly admit fallibility for trying to make people's lives 'straight.'

The act of repentance, what Jeremy M. Bergen calls "Ecclesial Repentance," is a public act. He says, "When acts of repentance include an apology or a request for forgiveness, there is an explicitly dialogical moment in which the Church awaits a response from those affected by its actions."[8] When the Church humbly seeks forgiveness, it not only experiences the grace of *being* forgiven but also appropriates the power to absolve sins from itself to the violated ones. The Church moves from being a forgiving community to becoming a forgiven community. Bergen rightfully reminds us that the confessions of the Church need to be public because its violations have been public. Such an act alone would pave way for reconciliation and healing. If the Church fails to interrogate itself, its spirituality and activism would be mere rhetoric and the practical efficacy of the Church's theology and mission would be stunted.

The "Body of Christ", The Queer Church

Elizabeth Stuart opines that, "... the Church is the only community under a mandate to be queer..."[9] Speaking of the body of Jesus, Graham Ward states how events of incarnation, transfiguration, crucifixion and resurrection suggest queerness in the body of Jesus. Jesus, a male, comes to life only from female matter implying a "complex web of symbolic relationships."[10] The transfigured body becomes transparent to divinity, and in the Eucharist Jesus' body from being male becomes gender-neutral in the form of bread. This bread—the body of Jesus—crosses cultural, sexual and gender boundaries. Ward notes that the crucified body, which becomes liminal, and the resurrected body, which reveals the mystery of the body, point to the "multi-gendered body of Christ."[11] What Stuart and Ward indicate is that queer is the ontological nature of the body of Christ, biological and metaphorical. Feminist theologians have challenged the use of exclusive language in theological discourses due to its ability to reinforce sexist culture, but Stuart asserts that such gender-specific language may actually be helpful in queering the Church—the body of Christ—where women being addressed as "men" and "brothers" and men becoming the "bride" of Christ neutralises the power that sex and gender have on human bodies.[12]

Ward in his article "There Is No Sexual Difference," presents a moment of queerness in the relationship between Jesus and Thomas. Jesus, post resurrection, invites Thomas to touch and examine his body (wounds). Thomas, in acknowledging Jesus' invitation, treads where no one has gone—into the very flesh of Jesus. Important to note is the communication between two same-sexed bodies as through this form of communication the two bodies become sexualised and queered.[13] The question one might ask now is: How is this relevant to envisioning a queer Church? The understanding of the displacement of Jesus' body and the *queer* moment between Jesus and Thomas (a moment of sexual friendship)[14] suggest that notions of sexual desire, difference, and bodily expressions can be queered with the hope of creating a community that celebrates this queerness. It is a deliberate move to interpret Church as the "body of Christ" and not as a physical, structural space. When members of the LGBTQ+ community become part of this body (not that they are not already), their queer bodies and queer identities queer the body of Christ, resulting in a transformed community whose identity emerges out of this continuous process of queering. This community reifies sexual friendship and diversity of identities and sexualities making the relationship between the queer God and the queer community fluid, mutual, and dynamic. If the Church in any way hopes of becoming a safe space for lesbians, gays, bisexuals and transpersons, it has to embody queerness. Becoming queer not only means becoming a community comprising of persons of diverse identities and sexualities, but becoming a community that absorbs the very essence of queerness in all of its being.

Church as a Rainbow Community

The rainbow has come to be associated with the LGBTQ+ community as it reflects queer identity and solidarity.[15] In his article "The Rainbow Connection: Bridging Asian American and Queer Theologies," Cheng mentions three interesting characteristics of the rainbow: multiplicity, diaspora and hybridity. He elucidates how the rainbow signifies multiple things and is interpreted in multiple ways depending on the respective culture. Furthermore, he notes that multiplicity refers to the multiple oppressions the LGBTQ+ communities face.[16] Multiplicity is therefore embodied in the rainbow and in queer communities. The second characteristic—diaspora—

implies how queer people experience "a profound sense of metaphorical homelessness."[17] Because of their sexuality and their 'inability' to fit into the system, queer people find themselves in "middle spaces." And finally, hybridity points to how queer people, particularly those with multiple racial and ethnic identities, live in a third space created by the "intersections of… sexualities on the one hand, and… racial identities on the other."[18] Sexual identities and racial identities are not mutually-exclusive categories, Cheng remarks.

The third characteristic seems relevant in the Indian context, not that others are not. In relation to the controversial 1996 movie *Fire,* Naisargi N. Dave states how the Hindu right wing argued that the two identities, "lesbian" and "Indian," could not become one. To her, the movie brought about "cultural anxiety about the moral meaning of the nation."[19] To fuse the two identities is to create an illusion of a nation that unites two mutually exclusive categories. This goes against the "Spirit of the Nation" as the nation is hetero-patriarchal, and nationalism is equivalent to heterosexism (interpreted in the line of Hindutva's ideology).[20] For Dave, uniting the two identities were "… a move in part to transform the nation by expanding the terms of its sexual citizenry."[21] What is the takeaway here? The queer subjects, in this case lesbians, were rendered non-citizens by the dominant due to their sexual orientation (because homosexuality is still considered by many to be a Western product). This is why the symbol of rainbow, particularly in its reference to hybridity, becomes such a powerful image as it helps undo binary thinking.

The Church, in becoming a rainbow community, will learn to respect difference in relational terms and celebrate the splendour of diversity and plurality. Here, characteristics such as multiplicity and hybridity will become sacred, and multiple retellings of experiences and multiple expressions of desire will be recognised and honoured.

Where is the Sexual, Indecent Church?

Nelson argues that the Church, throughout history, has been a sexual community. He states that when a child is welcomed into the body of Christ through baptism, the sexual relationship of the parents is recognised and celebrated.[22] Similarly, churches in India also celebrate adolescence as a means by which children attain sexual maturity. In recognising the sexuality and the sexual maturity of persons, the Church becomes a community of sexual beings. But just this is not what makes the Church a sexual community. The exigencies for a sexually provocative community demand the Church to stand up for sexual justice, disarm anti-sex dualisms within faith traditions and reimagine a spirituality that is pro-sex. If God is sexual and humans are sexual, then the relationship between the divine and human needs to be sexual and that forms the core of human spirituality.

Marcela Althaus-Reid, in arguing that theology is birthed within a hetero-patriarchal setting, uses the term "indecent" as a prefix to theology, suggesting that theology ought to be *indecent*. She uses this negatively-connoted word subversively, arguing that what is decent and indecent is constructed by the colonial world to control and authorise the social order.

To her the term indecent, being both political and erotic, contributes in the construction of sexual identities. Stressing on how the term is used (only) on women and persons of other sexual orientations, which is solely in relation to their sexual experience or inexperience, Althaus-Reid states that "indecency" upon subversion is the only way by which transformation can occur in Christianity.[23] I believe a Church modelled after an "indecent" morality can hope to change power relationships and the existing unjust structures that cause harm and pain, not just to the LGBTQ+ communities but to all humanity. An indecent body of Christ living out an indecent faith is deeply provocative.

Drawing inspiration from Althaus-Reid, De La Torre proposes an ethics that "screws" with the prevailing power structures.[24] Provocative, right? By provocative, I imply that the Church ought to challenge oppressive structures and those in power. The caste system is one such structure in the Indian context. It promulgates the concept of purity and pollution just as much as it needs the concept for its survival. This concept, regrettably, has been assumed by the Church as well. Gustavo Gutierrez once said in his sermon: "We don't need a Church of the pure."[25] In a context where people have for centuries been labelled "unclean," "impure," and "polluted" for their colour, gender, sexuality and non/ caste identity, a pure Church is out of the question. The need of the hour is an impure Church that provokes the assumed purity of the system.

As Althaus-Reid opines that every theology is a sexual act, the Church needs to be sexual in its ideologies and theologies; needs to be indecent in betraying sexual hierarchies and in being "illegitimate to the dominant norms and morality;"[26] and needs to be provocative, controversial and offensive in challenging ecclesial and civic authorities and eliminating unjust systems within the Church and outside. A sexually indecent Church will challenge the illegitimation of multiple sexual expressions of bodies and persons.

"Transformation is radically unsettling," claim James R. Oraker and Janis Hahn, for we are accustomed to a "static and predictable state."[27] Yet, this is the challenge before the Church. As Zachariah says, "We can either continue to remain as an inhospitable religious club… or we can become a just and inclusive rainbow community…."[28] The relevance of today's Church depends on its morally active commitment to promoting life and freedom and standing in solidarity with the most affected.

The Indian Church needs to be unsettled from its hetero-patriarchal foundations for sexual justice to be realised. It must listen and learn from the LGBTQ+ community to be a safe and affirming space. It must embody vulnerability and let queer folks reorient and reorder the body of Christ. In this process, the Church would painfully, yet liberatively, transform into a disruptive body of believers whose faith, in being disruptive, would spoil the normalisation of any form of injustice and re/affirm the sacramentality of sexuality.

Endnotes

1 "Pope Francis says Christians 'must apologize' to gay people," *DW*, https://www.dw.com/en/pope-francis-says-christians-must-apologize-to-gay-people/a-19358739 (accessed June 9, 2020).

2 Frederico Pieper Pires, "Liberation Theology, Modernity and Sexual Difference," in *Liberation Theology and Sexuality*, ed. Marcela Althaus-Reid (Hampshire: Ashgate Publishing Limited, 2006), 112.

3 It seems appropriate to make a mention of a queer reading of the parable of the Good Samaritan to highlight how inclusivity embodies notions of triumphalism. The conventional reading of the parable is in the Church identifying with the Good Samaritan and the queer community as the wounded victim who receives help from the Church. Paul Lakeland challenges this reading and tells us to reverse the roles, where queer Christians (and I add queer people of other faiths) are the Good Samaritans who help the Church, the wounded victim, find healing and transformation (the Church as a victim must be nuanced, he cautions). Here, the Church is the recipient and not the giver. Lakeland, in offering this new interpretation, challenges the conventional reading of the parable as the Church becomes too "self-congratulatory, over identifying with the Good Samaritan's heroic qualities…." This, he adds, is "at worst triumphalist and at best a sort of paternalistic vision…." The point Lakeland and I, in different ways of course, are making is that inclusivity embodies the concept of triumphalism and this is detrimental to queer communities. See, Paul Lakeland, "'I Want to Be in That Number': Desire, Inclusivity and the Church," in *Proceedings of the Catholic Theological Society of America*, 66 (2011): 21-27. Cited in, Sara Rosenau, "Queer Church: Failure and Becoming in the Body of Christ," in *Unlocking Orthodoxies for Inclusive Theologies*, eds. Robert E. Shore-Goss and Joseph N. Goh (London/New York: Routledge, 2020), 46-47.

4 Romal Laisram, interviewed by the author, Bangalore, March 9, 2017.

5 Marvin M. Ellison and Sylvia Thorson-Smith, "Wrestling to Dismantle Christian Homophobia and Heterosexism," in *Disruptive Faith, Inclusive Communities: Church and Homophobia*, eds. George Zachariah and Vincent Rajkumar (Bangalore/Delhi: CISRS/ISPCK, 2015), 209.

6 Frederico Pieper Pires, "Liberation Theology, Modernity and Sexual Difference," in *Liberation Theology and Sexuality*, 113-114.

7 Divya, interviewed by the author, Bangalore, March 4, 2017.

8 Jeremy M. Bergen, *Ecclesial Repentance: The Churches Confront their Sinful Pasts* (New York: T&T Clark International, 2011), 17.

[9] Elizabeth Stuart, "Sacramental Flesh," in *Queer Theology: Rethinking the Western Body*, ed. by Gerard Loughlin (Victoria: Blackwell Publishing Ltd., 2007), 65.

[10] Graham Ward, "Bodies: The Displaced Body of Jesus Christ," in *Radical Orthodoxy: A New Theology*, eds. John Milbank, Catherine Pickstock and Graham Ward (New York: Taylor & Francis e-Library, 2002), 165.

[11] Graham Ward, "Bodies: The Displaced Body of Jesus Christ," in *Radical Orthodoxy*, 176.

[12] Graham Ward, "Bodies: The Displaced Body of Jesus Christ," in *Radical Orthodoxy*, 72.

[13] Graham Ward, "There Is No Sexual Difference," in *Queer Theology: Rethinking the Western Body*, ed. by Gerard Loughlin (Victoria: Blackwell Publishing Ltd., 2007), 81-82.

[14] Sexual friendship, insists Mary Hunt, embodies mutuality and intimacy and not necessarily genitality. See, Mary E. Hunt, "Friends in Deed," in *Sex and God: Some Varieties of Women's Religious Experience*, ed. Linda Hurcombe (New York: Routledge & Kegan Paul), 1987. Cited in, Adrian Thatcher, *Liberating Sex: A Christian Sexual Theology* (London: SPCK, 1993), 168.

[15] Curtis M. Wong says the rainbow flag and its colours are interpreted differently by different groups and outlets. However, according to queer artist Gilbert Baker, the one who designed the rainbow flag in 1978 and never copyrighted it as he wanted every queer person to own it, pink stands for sex, red for life, orange for healing, yellow for sunlight, green for nature, turquoise for magic, indigo for harmony, and violet for spirit. Over the years, colours have been replaced and removed. Today, the most common flag is one with six colours, where turquoise and violet have been replaced by blue (harmony) and purple (spirit) respectively, and pink is removed. Curtis M. Wong, "The History and Meaning of The Rainbow Pride Flag," *Huffpost*,

https://www.huffpost.com/entry/rainbow-pride-flag-history_n_5b193aafe4b 0599bc6e124a0 (accessed June 11, 2020).

[16] Patrick S. Cheng, "The Rainbow Connection: Bridging Asian American and Queer Theologies," *Theology & Sexuality*, 17:3 (2011): 238-239.

[17] Patrick S. Cheng, "The Rainbow Connection: Bridging Asian American and Queer Theologies," 244.

[18] Patrick S. Cheng, "The Rainbow Connection: Bridging Asian American and Queer Theologies," 246.

[19] Naisargi N. Dave, *Queer Activism in India: A Story in the Anthropology of Ethics* (London: Duke University Press, 2012), 149.

[20] Hindu nationalists consider "nation" as a woman that deserves respect, honour and protection. This not only accentuates men's masculinity, but

demands women to order their lives within the nationalist heterosexist framework. A woman may be considered a citizen only when she abides by the ideals of motherhood and womanhood Hindu nationalists propose. The "lesbian" identity becomes diabolical and repulsive as it circumvents male chauvinist Hindu nationalist structure.

[21] Naisargi N. Dave, *Queer Activism in India: A Story in the Anthropology of Ethics*, 162.

[22] James B. Nelson, *Embodiment: An Approach to Sexuality and Christian Theology*, 251.

[23] Marcela Althaus-Reid, *Indecent Theology: Theological Perversion in Sex, Gender and Politics* (London: Routledge, 2000), 168-170.

[24] Miguel De La Torre proposes an ethics of *para joder* and the Spanish word *joder* means "to screw with." Talk about ethics being provocative! See, Miguel De La Torre, "Jesús: Welcoming the Indecent," *Liberating Sexuality: Justice Between the Sheets*, 197.

[25] Joshua J. McElwee, "Gutierrez at Vatican: Church must be Samaritan, reaching out to others," *National Catholic Reporter*,

https://www.ncronline.org/blogs/ncr-today/gutierrez-vatican-church-must-be-samaritan-reaching-out-others (accessed June 10, 2020).

[26] George Zachariah, "Introduction," in *Disruptive Faith, Inclusive Communities: Church and Homophobia*, xxix.

[27] James R. Oraker and Janis Hahn, "The Church in Action Asking Hard Questions," *Out of the Shadows into the Light: Christianity and Homosexuality*, ed. Miguel A. De La Torre (St. Louis: Chalice Press, 2009), 121.

[28] George Zachariah, "Church: A Rainbow Community of the Beloved and Equals," https://www.academia.edu/2644190/Church_A_Rainbow_Community_of_the_Beloved_and_Equals (accessed June 9, 2020).

What is the Sin of Sodom?

Genesis 19 is a text that is familiar to us. Two (male) angels arrive at Sodom, and Lot invites them to his house. Though the men refuse at first, preferring to rest in the city square, they agree to go to Lot's house. While they are at home, the men of the city of Sodom make their way to Lot's house and demand that the two men be sent out so they can have sex with them. Lot attempts to negotiate with them by offering his two daughters, but the men of the city refuse to accept his 'gracious' offer. As negotiations fail, the two men drag Lot inside and strike the townsmen with blindness. The next morning, God destroys Sodom and Gomorrah.

Now most of us have heard, if not preached, that God destroyed Sodom and Gomorrah for its practice of homosexuality. While Genesis 19 has been used to demonise lesbians and gays, it is noteworthy that there is absolutely no direct reference to homosexuality at all. When the text is read with the previous chapter as the background, one realises that the sin of Sodom is not homosexuality but rather inhospitality to the two men, the messengers or guests.[1] Verses such as Ezekiel 16:49 and Amos 4:1 and 11 tell us that God's wrath came upon the people of Sodom due to their refusal to do justice to orphans, widows and the needy. Hospitality, during biblical times, was not just an ethical imperative for communities but also, and importantly, a divine command. Even Jesus makes a reference to Sodom in Luke 10. To the people that refused to welcome the seventy (or seventy-two), Jesus says, "[I]t will be more bearable on that day for Sodom than for that town" (Luke 10:12). The emphasis is on inhospitality.

Though scholars and theologians have come to agree that Genesis 19 is indeed about inhospitality and not homosexuality, it remains a rather weak argument. What then must one make of the text? Verse 5 reads: "Bring them out to us, so that we may know them" (NRSV). The townsmen's demand *to know* the guests suggests that there is a sexual connotation to it, because the word *yada* meaning "to know" is a euphemism for sexual intercourse. One could then argue that the real issue in Genesis 19 is not homosexuality nor inhospitality but rather same-sex gang rape by heterosexual men.[2]

A distinction must be made between sex and rape. The purpose of rape is not sexual fulfilment but the humiliation of the Other. It is not consensual. For Barbara Sichtermann, rape is ultimately an act that involves the domination and loathing of the Other. The men of the city wanted to have sex with the two male guests as a symbolic act of humiliation. Their desire was to conquer and subdue the Other; it was not a desire borne out of love or for that matter lust. The need to rape the guests was to reinforce their control and reinstate their superiority over the Other. That is why the men of the city say of Lot: "This fellow came here as an alien, and he would play the judge" (verse 9). And on saying it, they proceeded towards Lot himself. It is pretty evident that the Sodomites were not homosexuals but self-indulgent, xenophobic men.[3]

Sexual injustice occurs when feelings of control and violence supersede mutual erotic expressions. This is clearly reflected in the text. The men did not exhibit a passionate desire for the two male guests. If it were, one could make a case about homosexuality or homoeroticism. But there is no reference to a desire of that kind. The men clearly wanted to humiliate the two men who were not from the same town. They also took the opportunity to give Lot, who was a resident alien himself, a hard time. Rather than choosing to affirm and welcome diversity and different identities, the men sought to commit indignity on the two guests. Genesis 19 is a classic example of sexual injustice.

Endnotes

[1] Monica Jyotsna Melanchthon, "Sexuality," in *Created in God's Image: From Hegemony to Partnership,* eds. Patricia Sheerattan-Bisnauth and Philip Vinod Peacock (Geneva: WCC, 2010), 165.

[2] Barbara Sichtermann, "Rape and Sexuality," in *The Polity Reader in Gender Studies* (Cambridge: Polity Press, 2002), 278.

[3] John Corvino, *What's Wrong with Homosexuality?* (New York: Oxford University Press, 2013), 29-30.

Queering John 21:
Peter and Jesus in Conversation

One of the purposes of a queer reading is to unearth queer identities. With the help of Robert Goss' strategy of outing the text, I attempt to locate queerness in the characters involved in John 21. In this pericope, Jesus asks Peter three times, "Do you love me…?" Each time Peter responds in the affirmative (verses 15-17). The Greek language becomes rather significant for us here. While Jesus asks Peter if he loves him with an *agape* love, Peter on all three occasions responds affirmatively with a *philia* love. Only the third time does Jesus change his words to *philia* love. While Peter has often been accused of not understanding Jesus' question and not loving him with an *agape* love, Peter's response, I believe, actually exposes his own queerness and Jesus' vulnerability to it. Let me explain.

D.A. Carson notes that Peter uses the weaker form of love, i.e., *philia* as against the stronger form of love, i.e., *agape*, for he believes that Peter has his "old self-confidence expunged from him."[1] Carson, I suppose, comes to this conclusion believing Peter to be troubled by the events of his denial of Jesus or perhaps the crucifixion itself. Though this could be a possibility, it is my opinion that Peter deliberately refers to *philia* love. Perhaps, Peter's use of the 'weaker' form of love is in a way calling Jesus to embrace his own vulnerability by loving with a 'weak' love. Vulnerability is often seen as weakness, thereby causing men to avoid it. But if men embrace vulnerability, the desire for bonding and expressions of emotional intimacy become possible. Peter, by refusing to answer in *agape* love, which in being philanthropic and altruistic negates emotional attachment, draws Jesus to a place of vulnerability.

What makes *philia* love a vulnerable form of love or, by extension, queer? *Philia* love, Kenneth Wuest says, is a love that is called out of one's heart as a response to the pleasure one takes in a person or object.[2] The word *philia* also occurs in John 11:3 and 11: 36. When Jesus wept outside the tomb of Lazarus, the Jews on seeing him weep said, "See how he loved him!" (11:36). The love referred to here is *philia*. This suggests that there is something powerful and evocative about a *philia* love that caused Jesus to weep (11:35). It was a kind of love that drew Jesus to the tomb to bring Lazarus back to life, as he could not stand being separated from him. Does Lazarus respond affirmatively to Jesus' *philia* love by "coming out"?[3] You bet he does! Similarly, Peter's *philia* love for Jesus was a committed, affectionate and a chosen love. Somehow Jesus, I suspect, was slow in grasping that. By expressing his *philia* love to Jesus three times, Peter draws Jesus to embrace vulnerability and be willing to love and be loved back by Peter's *philia* love, thereby 'rejecting' the hierarchical *agape* love. Jesus' decision to change his question from *agape* to *philia* on the third occasion can be seen as an affirmative response to Peter's love.

The experience of vulnerability and acceptance are evident in Peter and Jesus. This is a sign of a mutually fulfilling sexual friendship. Sexual friendship, insists Mary Hunt, embodies mutuality and intimacy and not necessarily genitality.[4] Adrian Thatcher, likewise, notes that sexual friendships honour vulnerability as an expression of love.[5] The difficulty in accepting the text as pointing to queerness can arise with the use of *philia* love as against *eros*. Yet, can the lines between *philia* and *eros* be blurred? If all are created as sexual beings and have the inherent need for communion and intimacy, same-sex and cross-sex friendships are not unnatural. Peter, in the text, is seen seeking validation, love and affection from Jesus, and there is nothing wrong in that. (Remember James Nelson's observation that heterosexual men are repelled by gays because gays seek validation from other men?). I do not make the claim that Jesus and Peter were gay—this would be imposing a modern category to bygone characters. Sexual friendship merely alludes to homoeroticism, which need not involve genitality. A queer reading of the text helps unearth queer identities and makes the text alive.

Endnotes

[1] D.A. Carson, *The Gospel According to John* (Michigan: William B. Eerdmans Publishing Company, 1991), 676.

[2] Kenneth Wuest, *Wuest's Word Studies in the Greek New Testament,* vol. III (Michigan: William. B. Eerdmans Publishing Co., 1975), 62-63.

[3] Marcela Althaus-Reid, *Indecent Theology: Theological Perversions in Sex, Gender and Politics*, 114.

[4] Mary E. Hunt, "Friends in Deed," *Sex and God: Some Varieties of Women's Religious Experience*, ed. Linda Hurcombe (New York: Routledge & Kegan Paul), 1987. Cited in, Adrian Thatcher, *Liberating Sex: A Christian Sexual Theology* (London: SPCK, 1993), 168.

[5] Adrian Thatcher, *Liberating Sex*, 168.

The 'Pride' Journey: Where Sexuality and Spirituality Meet

Having in mind the issues surrounding the LGBTQ+ communities in India, I am trying to reinterpret Matthew 2:1-12 by 'queering' the Star of the East, and relating it to the Pride Walk that takes place every year in India. I take the Wise Men to represent the LGBTQ+ community. What then is the Star? Amidst the countless stars around, there was this one star that stood out bright, drawing the Wise Men to a place of spirituality. The star that shone the brightest did have a 'queer' brightness to it so much so that the Wise Men, finding it rather 'strange,' chose to *explore* it. I take the star to signify sexuality. The Wise Men, on seeing, experiencing and wanting to explore the star, decided to 'come out' of their closets (their place of dwelling) and began the journey of understanding and discovering the mystery of the star. i.e., their own sexualities, with their *telos* being spirituality, the worship of their liberator. However, that purpose almost vanquished when they came in contact with King Herod, who, in a sense, represents the hetero-patriarchal structures of society that continue to mock, victimise and slay the LGBTQ+ communities in the name of religion. Just as our sexualities bridge God and us, the star eventually bridged them and their liberator.

Every year, the LGBTQ+ communities in Bengaluru come out to participate in the Pride Walk. While it is a time of protest against the injustices done to them, it is also a time of celebration, a celebration of their sexualities that give them identity and meaning. I believe people out there at some point in their life saw that star, wondered what it was, and knowing that the journey of discovery would be hard and long chose to 'explore' it. The Pride Walk is similar to the Pride Journey of the Wise Men. This rarely happens in solitude: the men in the narrative needed each other much like the LGBTQ+ communities need each other. And just the way the Wise Men found an alternative path back home, these communities are always treading on new paths, dismantling and disturbing heteronormativity. We have often been told that our lives must parallel that of the Wise Men. Perhaps, it is time for us to listen to and learn from our LGBTQ+ friends for they, upon embracing the mystery of the star, show us a sacred space—a sacred space where sexuality and spirituality converge.

Envisioning an Inclusive Church[1]

The 2009 Delhi High Court verdict and the subsequent Supreme Court verdicts on Section 377 of the Indian Penal Code initiated intense discussions and deliberations in India on human sexuality. Religious leaders have challenged these verdicts aggressively in the name of culture, tradition and family values. Various church bodies passed resolutions condemning the verdict. On the other hand, the hitherto silenced sexual minorities who have been forced to confine to the closets, along with their allies, celebrated the verdicts for decriminalising their lives. In such a context of moral ambiguity and conflicting standpoints, it is important for the members of the body of Christ to reflect upon the implications of these verdicts for the being and the becoming of the Church in India. How do we become a Church to those brothers and sisters who are ostracised and excluded from the fuller communion of the Church? How can the Church reclaim its vision of a rainbow community of the beloved and equals?

The Church has always approached homosexuality as a moral issue and has been reluctant to welcome and include homosexuals into faith communities. Most churches reject homosexuality as sinful and immoral unconditionally and refuse sacraments and ordination to people with homosexual orientations. In the case of some churches, they condemn homosexuality but not the homosexual person based on the principle "hate the sin; love the sinner." There are also people who consider homosexuality not as a matter of sexual orientation, but choice. They consider homosexuality as an addiction, from which the person can be saved by coming to Jesus. The role of the Church in such situations is to help lesbians and gays to change their sinfulness and abnormality by turning back to Jesus. Finally, there are also a few churches that understand same-sex relations as capable of expressing God's purposes, and lesbians and gays as people with dignity created in the image of God. All these diverse standpoints reveal that the Church is not a welcoming place to people who are not straight.

The Bible plays a significant role in discerning our response to homosexuality. Many of us tend to believe that "homosexuality is sinful because the Bible says so." What the Bible teaches about homosexuality is the question that we need to ask in order to make an opinion on this issue. This question does not recognise the importance of hermeneutics in understanding biblical texts. It stems from the dominant idea of biblical interpretation as an objective scientific study to dig out the original meaning of the original author buried in the text. We tend to believe that this approach of reading the Bible is an innocent, unbiased and scientific method with universal validity. This approach, however, has been contested by readings from the margins.

The Bible has played a significant role in violence inflicted upon sexual minorities. This experience of scriptural violence has compelled many lesbians and gays to hate the Bible and to leave the Church. But the biblical abuse initiated by the heterosexist interpretations has also led to the emergence of queer interpretative communities who read the Bible from their standpoint to protect themselves from scripturally sanctioned violence and exclusion. Their attempt to "take back the Word" has not only protected them but also enabled them to celebrate their lives.

Queer biblical interpretation has two functions. On the one hand, it attempts to critique heterosexist interpretations that use Bible to condemn homosexuality and legitimise and perpetuate the exclusion of and violence against sexual minorities. On the other hand, it is also a positive reading strategy to reclaim the Bible and to rediscover the subjectivity within the Bible. One of the positive methods of queer interpretations is known as "befriending the text." Even as we commit ourselves to transform our faith communities into just and inclusive communities, let us try to draw inspiration from Bible using the method of befriending the text to enable and empower us for this great task.

In befriending the text, the text of homosexual lives interacts with the text of scripture. "The point of reference for a queer reading of scripture is the notion that the Bible is our friend. When we approach the Bible as a friendly text, as a text that 'does not harm,' the terror of the scripture is transformed into the life-giving word of God. We are able to find our story within it." Befriending the text is a deep spiritual experience for sexual minorities because it enables them to affirm that "we too have been graciously invited to God's inclusive table; and we are taking back the word as we take back our Christian practices."

The epistle to the Ephesians is addressed to a multicultural church, primarily with Jewish and Hellenistic communities. The epistle talks about the unity and reconciliation of the whole people of God through the agency of the Church. So the Church, in the letter to the Ephesians, is an inclusive Church that celebrated diversity and differences. What is the theological reason for imagining the Church as an inclusive community in a multicultural and pluralistic context? Is it just an attempt to be politically correct, or is there a theological rationale to argue that the Church is essentially an inclusive community?

First of all, Christian faith that affirms one body, one spirit, one hope, one Lord, one faith, one baptism, and one God is not a rejection of diversities; rather, it is an affirmation of the reconciliation of all diversities in Christ. Plurality and diversity are not accidents or deformities that need to be cured and treated. The reconciled diversity that we find in the one Lord, or one body, or one spirit, or one baptism is not the imposition of a particular worldview or practice or sexual orientation as normative for all. Rather, as members of the one body, sharing the same baptismal vow of allegiance to the one Lord, our differences are being reconciled in Christ Jesus. So inclusiveness is not a choice that the Church ought to make. Inclusiveness is the basic characteristic of the Church. A Church with fortified walls practising untouchability towards people who share the same image of God and who are marked by the sign of cross in the sacrament of baptism cannot be considered as the Church of Christ. The Church of Christ is a Church without walls, extending its fellowship to all those who are loved by God in Christ Jesus.

Second, our calling as Christians is not to exclude but to practice the spirit of reconciliation for unity in the bond of love and peace. The author of the epistle reminds us that, "I therefore, beg you to lead a life worthy of the calling to which you have been called, with all humility and gentleness, with patience, bearing with one another in love, making every effort to maintain the unity of the spirit in the bond of peace." So if all our diversities are reconciled in Christ, then our calling is to lead a life worthy of this divine purpose of reconciliation for which God has called us. Often, we exclude others out of our desire to become a holy people by condemning them as immoral and impure. But once again we are reminded that holiness is not something that we achieve by sanitising and insulating ourselves from the sinful world; holiness is an invitation to become holy in the way of Jesus, the Christ. Holiness for Jesus meant challenging the purity maps of his time which excluded people on the basis of their health, ethnicity, class nature and gender status. In that process he touched leprosy-affected people, he touched the ears and eyes of people with deformities, he touched human saliva, he dined with socially outcast people, he protected "notorious" women, and he was crucified outside the city gates. By touching the untouchables, Jesus inaugurated God's reign in our midst. The Church is duty-bound to continue this mission of touching the untouchables. Christian mission of reconciliation presupposes the prophetic courage to touch the untouchables. The Church becomes first fruits of the reign of God only when we respond to this call in the bond of love and peace and welcome into our midst those who are condemned as untouchables.

Third, the Church is called to speak the truth in love to grow into the fullness of Christ. Speaking the truth in love is a difficult task. Speaking the truth that in Christ we are all reconciled with one another is a dangerous proposition. We are still reluctant to recognise casteism as the original sin of our country because we are afraid to speak the truth in love. We continue to be comfortable in excluding women from the total life of the Church because we are not yet ready to speak the truth in love. Our homophobia against people with different sexual orientations exposes our unwillingness to speak the truth in love. Speaking the truth in love demands from us the courage to expose the untruth of our dominant truth claims. Exposing our untruths is an invitation to a costly *metanoia*: a *metanoia* to transform our faith communities from an obsession with the prevailing dominant truth claims of our times to discover in love new truths—truths that compel us to grow into the fullness of Christ. Growing into the fullness of Christ enables the Church to grow in love. From the fear of the unknown, the stranger, and the person who is different from us, we grow into the beauty of the rainbow where we celebrate the splendour of beauty without sacrificing our differences.

If this is the Gospel of Jesus, the Christ, we see the manifestation of the same Gospel in the judgment in 2009 of the learned judges of the Delhi High Court with regard to decriminalising homosexuality. Chief Justice A.P. Shah and Justice S. Murlidhar, in their historic verdict, made a distinction between public morality and constitutional morality. Public morality is informed by dominant social norms and values. Constitutional morality, on the other hand, envisions the highest ethical principles. Public morality is what the dominant system prescribes as good and moral. Legitimising laws in the name of public morality is unethical as it prevents the possibility of the blossoming of constitutional morality. Again, the rationale for the judges to affirm constitutional morality above public morality was the principle of inclusiveness, the underlying theme of the Indian Constitution. As followers of the nonconformist Christ—the one who consistently quarrelled with the priests of public morality—our call is to reject all laws that demonise, criminalise and exclude human beings from the total life of the Church and society.

This calls for corrections in the prevailing power inequities in the Church and society. Social and cultural norms have to be reimagined so that differences in caste, gender and sexuality are no longer ranked hierarchically in terms of superiority and inferiority. Differences should not be occasions for domination but for recognising and validating variations within a richly diverse humanity.

"A prayer of lament" articulates the agony of a person with different sexual orientation: "Let me have a share of your peace without obsessing that my 'lifestyle' is not Christian, without hating myself, my fate, my body, and my heart. Let me live a life of joy and peace, secure in the knowledge that your grace fills me, that nothing I have done or desired or worried about can erase your love for me that you bid me come 'just as I am.'"

This is the vision of a rainbow community of the beloved and equals. The Indian Church has two options: we can either continue to remain as an inhospitable religious club—a hostile community as the rapists of Sodom in Genesis 19, committing violence against sexual minorities, or we can become a just and inclusive rainbow community celebrating our God-given diversities by welcoming those who are different from us into our midst to experience Christian fellowship in a deeper way. God of love has called us as a community of friends and equals to be filled with God's love; to share God's unconditional love; to demonstrate God's love to others—whoever they are, whatever their background be; to declare and show by our actions that God loves all, and has no pre-existing conditions for loving all of God's creations. May the God of love help us to become a Church to those who are demonised, criminalised and excluded.

Endnotes

[1] The Bible study is contributed by George Zachariah, Wesley Lecturer in Theological Studies, Trinity Methodist Theological College, Auckland, Aotearoa New Zealand.

Liturgy 1

Redeeming Masculinity, Building Affirmative Communities[1]

Taizé Chant: Stay with us O Lord Jesus Christ, night will soon fall. Then stay with us O Lord Jesus Christ, light in our darkness (led by the Choir)

Breaking the Silence:

(Voice 1) *I have no shelter, no respite, nowhere to run from this vile society that constantly torments me. I have nothing left of me to go on. Is there someone who can rescue me?*

(Voice 2) *I have been persecuted by my fellowmen for not being the real 'man' that I was expected to be. I feel humiliated. Is there someone to accept me the way I am?*

Call to Encounter God:

Come together and discern God's love, **a love that heals deep scars.**

Come together and witness God's power, **a power that embodies freedom and life.**

Come together and experience God's Shalom, **a Shalom that bridges all amidst differences.**

Come let us worship the Source of life, the Living Word and the Abiding Spirit

We have come to worship the Triune God.

Prayer to 'be with us':

God of all creation, who unites us in the midst of varied natures of masculine and feminine persona, accept our worship. As we seek your guidance, disturb our spirits and restore in us the newness of vision, the optimism of hope, and the vigour of action. In Jesus' name we pray, **Amen.**

Song of Praise and Hope:[2] *(To be sung in the tune of "Nearer My God to Thee")*

1.   We come just as we are, our hearts long for you
       In our low estate, we'll still hope in you
       We lift our voice to you, Lord, will you hear our song?
       In our deepest hour, we will still praise you.

2.   We live our lives between fire and the flame
       Waves sweep across our land; our world needs you now.
       But we know deep within, you'll be our only hope
       We've come just as we are, won't you hear our song?

The Word of God: 2 Samuel 11:2-5 and 14-17

Preparatory Song:[3]
Ancient Words ever true, changing me and changing you. We have come with open hearts, oh let the Ancient Words impart.

A Time for Introspection: Redeeming Masculinity, Building Affirmative Communities

Words of Penitence:

We want to see how you see, change our hearts Lord, make it holy; if there's anything in our lives that doesn't honour you today, we're listening Lord, speak to us, speak to us.[4]

(Men) God, forgive us for we men have created you in our image—an image that is ostracising, excluding others. We confess our shortcomings to you and pray for your forgiveness for having been a part in forming, elevating and enjoying the patriarchal privileges that distort your image. God of mercy, transform us, **Amen.**

(Women) God, give ear to the repenting men and grant them peace and forgiveness. We too seek your forgiveness for often remaining silent at the sight of injustice. God of mercy, transform us, **Amen.**

(Voices 1 & 2) *Your repentance is genuine, but will we be affirmed for who we are?*

Absolution:

I have heard your confession. I, in my tenderness and graciousness, grant you forgiveness and peace so that you may discern my call. **Amen.**

A Testimonial of our Faith:

We believe in the God, who shuns the mighty and lofty, defends the feeble and fragile, and who being the source of masculine and feminine persona affirms life in all; one who is outside of ourselves yet living within and conjoined with us.

We believe in Jesus, who being born of a virgin mother, never hesitated to shed tears, never claimed to be above another, and though being called the "Son of David," subverted the very idea of lordship and royalty and was subject to violence and murder; who by laying down his life and being raised up again revealed vulnerability and hope; and who is coming back again as one who still bears the marks of pain and assault, hence revelatory of the becoming.

We believe in the Holy Spirit, the *Ruah* that pierces through our spirit and convicts us, who is available for the tempted and the tried, and who creates communities of benevolent hope.

We believe in the Church, called to be the hands, the feet, and the voice of God; a body that advocates and celebrates diversities. Amen.

Prayers 'of and for' others:

(Voice 3) *I have been raised in a culture where my masculine traits were glorified and always endorsed to patriarchal values and virtues. I enjoyed that privilege. But now, I seek to be different and sensitive.*

Let us pray that men would realise that women and transpersons are also a reflection of God's image. Let them be gentle and kind in their relationships and not glorify their manhood.

(Voice 4) *Every day I witness women being subjected to inhuman acts, but I've always passed them by thinking of my own safety and well-being. But now, I seek to be different and responsive.*

Let us pray that women would stand up to confront injustice and work together to eliminate structures that perpetuate partisanship.

(Voice 5) *I was hostile towards those who I viewed as being 'lower' than me. I misused my position and dishonoured my people. But now, I seek to be different and receptive.*

Let us pray that the body of Christ will welcome all into its fold without prejudice and without succumbing to those social and cultural norms that are life-negating.

(Voice 6) *I vehemently opposed every attempt aimed at seeing the male as being equal to the rest. I desired control, power and authority. But now, I want to be different and discerning.*

Let us pray that the leaders of all nations will strive to uphold and affirm the dignity and freedom of every person, and challenge those structures that venerate the male.

Lord, in your mercy, **hear our prayer, Amen.**

Lord's Prayer:[5]
Our Creator in heaven
Reveal who you are
Set right the wrong
May your heart's desire be manifested on earth
Give us that which we need
You forgive us as we forgive others
Keep us safe from ourselves and the evil one
Be what you are

Let the power of your justice
And the glory of your love be established
You're ablaze in beauty
From eternity to eternity, Amen
(Voice 1 and 2) *Will you accept us and work towards keeping your commitment?*

All: Yes! As the Grace of God abides with us, we will continue to do so.

Commitment Song:[6] (*Let us all stand and join in with the Choir*)

1.   We will work for the good of each other
    We will walk in the path of your love
    We will celebrate the works of your hands
    We'll not defile what you've made.

Pre-Ch)   We open up our hearts to you
    Won't you change it and make it brand new?

Ch) *We will break every wall that divides*
    We'll make way, for your justice to reign
    Draw us near to celebrate each other
    We will sow seeds of love.

2.   We will cast every conceit and hate
    We will turn from what keeps us apart
    We will hold on to, to every good thing
    Seal us with your holy zeal.

Prayer to 'go with us':

God, our helper, we thank you for this time of devotion where we could reexamine our lives in the light of your Word. Save us from building altars to prejudice, injustice and patriarchy. May we work together to bring about a culture where all are affirmed and honoured. In Jesus' name we pray, Amen.

Benediction:

Let us be sure in what we do. Let us be wise in what we speak. Let us be just in what we pull down and build. In all our endeavours to witness affirming communities, let us be assured of God's grace and blessing, **Amen.**

Endnotes

[1] This liturgy was prepared by Arvind Theodore and was used for the worship service on the 12 August 2013 at the United Theological College, Bengaluru.

[2] Lyrics modified by the Worship Leader.

[3] Chorus of the Song titled "Ancient Words" by Lynn DeShazo. Taken from the album "Worship Again" by Michael W. Smith.

[4] Song titled "Speak to me" by Dave Luben from the album "A Place Called Surrender." Lyrics modified by the Worship Leader.

[5] The Lord's Prayer (taken from the Message Version) has been modified by the Worship Leader.

[6] The Song "Seeds of Love" is composed by the Worship Leader. You can listen to the song on YouTube by searching "Seeds of Love + Arvind Theodore".

Church: A Rainbow Community of the Beloved and Equals[1]

Invitation:

Come into this place of peace,

and let its silence heal your spirit.

Come into this place of memory,

and let its history warm your soul.

Come into this place of prophecy and power,

and let its vision change your heart.

Bhajan:

A Litany of Assurance:

It doesn't matter who you are or where you're coming from,

This Place has got an open door to make you feel at home.

And if you will come in and join us, you will soon perceive

That though we might all have our doubts,

there's something we believe.

The shape and form of every person comes from God's own hand;

And though you might not recognise it, or yet understand,

To all who see your deepest nature there's a sign that shows

You share a likeness with the One from whom all life arose.

This world may soil you or contort you, robbing you of pride,

And people leave you feeling small, with words aimed to deride,

Still nothing can defeat the truth that you derive from the One

who counts your worth today as much

as when you first were born.

So join your hands with ours and let us grow in self-respect.

And hear the story of a Friend who calls us to deep friendship and fellowship

That gives a healthy new-found confidence to let our spirit live.

Introspection:

We are your gay, lesbian, bisexual, and transgendered children:

You must not seek vengeance, nor bear a grudge against the children of your people. (Leviticus 19:18)

We are your bisexual, transgendered, lesbian, and gay parents:

Revere your mother and father, each one of you. (Leviticus 19:3)

We are elderly lesbians, bisexuals, gay men, and transgendered people:

You shall rise before the aged and show deference to the old. (Leviticus 19:32)

We are the stranger:

You must not oppress the stranger. You shall love the stranger as yourself, for you were strangers in the land of Egypt. (Leviticus 19:34)

We are your transgendered, gay, bisexual, and lesbian siblings:

You shall not hate your brother or sister in your heart. (Leviticus 19:17)

We are lesbian, gay, transgendered, and bisexual victims of gay-bashing and murder:

You may not stand idly when your neighbour's blood is being shed. (Leviticus 19:16)

We are your bisexual, gay, transgendered, and lesbian neighbors:

You must not oppress your neighbour. You must judge your neighbour justly. You shall love your neighbour as you love yourself. (Leviticus 19: 13, 15, 18)

Reconciliation:

A dove returns to the Ark, bearing in its beak the fresh leaf of an olive branch. "No more," God promises, "will I destroy the creatures I have created."

"It is finished," the Saviour cried in his last words—his work done, his ministry of reconciliation completed—upon the Cross. Throughout the scriptures, throughout the Church, the "bottom line" of our faith in God is the truth—for the sake of Jesus Christ—that we are reconciled. It is God's will that all be saved, and come to the knowledge of the truth.

"What is truth?" Above and beyond the teachings of Christian faith—whether very deep or utterly simply, whether in contention or consistent, open to debate, subject to interpretation—one truth rises: we are—all of us—reconciled in Christ, and in him we have life, light, joy and peace. In his reconciling love, let us sing, let God's unfailing love give us full voice.

Readings: Ephesians: 4: 1-16

Reflection: A Prayer of Lament

Affirmation of Faith: *(stand)*

We celebrate the unity we create in the midst of our diversity. We believe in God's creative, and embracing love for all that is. We affirm the inherent beauty, worth, and dignity of all human beings.
We believe that God does not make junk.

The choice is not whether to be gays, lesbians, transgendered, bisexual or straight, but whether or not to live an authentic life.

We believe God wants us to be reliable and trustworthy.

Coming out is a courageous and spiritual act.

We believe that God rejoices when we reveal to the world our full selves.

Sexual expression is one of the many sacred ways that consensual adults can express the depth of love in their relationships.

We believe God made sex good.

We support each person's journey of integrating spirituality and sexuality which leads to wholeness.

We believe God entwines body and spirit in all people.

Marriage is a sacred union for people who are committed to each other. Love and justice sustain the family.

We believe God wills life-long covenants of just-love.

No one is free when others are oppressed.

We believe God cries with the persecuted. The Crucified God is hidden in their sufferings and struggles. Their yearning for freedom is also God's.

Church is a rainbow community that affirms, welcomes, leads, protects, and celebrates diversity in God's creation.

We believe God inspires us to become a just and inclusive community.

Responsive Prayer: *(stand)*
Today, we are reminded of the inclusive spirit of community and family. We are grateful for relationships and solidarity.

We come together, knowing and living the diverse variety of family arrangements through centuries and cultures.
We rejoice in our imagination and resilience as we inspire each other to be families and communities for each generation.

We celebrate our family members and allies who have shown us unconditional love and also continue to grow in relationship with us.

We delight in our communities that support one another through life and death.

We feel grateful for our supportive siblings, our parents, our grandparents, our Friends—our families—who uphold us and bring us joy.

We gather to celebrate as community and as families, and also remember those in need of support, those who often feel alone and silenced.

With mindful hearts and assurance in the connectivity of this beautiful earth that is our home, we are thankful for the connection that extends beyond biology and heritage.

Together: Through this community that surrounds us, we experience the unity of humanity and creation. We now open ourselves to the healing and nurturing presence in this community gathered, knowing that it will be ours wherever we go.

Closing Hymn: *(stand)*
We shall overcome (2)
We shall overcome some day
Oh deep in our hearts, we do believe
We shall overcome someday

Hum honge kaamyaab, hum honge kaamyaab
hum honge kaamyaab ek din

ho mann main hai vishwas
poora hai vishwas
hum honge kaamyaab ek din.

Benediction: *(stand)*

Dearly beloved in Christ, let us bless each other. Let us continue our journey walking in love. Though there may be storms ahead, be encouraged. Know that you do not walk alone. Know that the simplicity of water can heal and renew. Know that the rock of relationships can foster growth. Care for one another and care for the earth. Seek justice and make peace in our families, churches, communities, nation, and the world. **Amen.**

Endnotes

[1] This is the order of worship that was used for the community worship service held on the 2 August 2009 at the Gurukul Lutheran Theological College and Research Institute, Chennai, on the wake of the Delhi High Court verdict on Section 377 of the Indian Penal Code.

http://indwellingspirit.org/prayers/

http://www.welcomingresources.org/affirmations.htm

http://www.netrj.org/resources/talkingcircle.html

Afterword

*John Lalnuntluanga**

The book *Church and Human Sexuality* authored by Arvind Theodore is an introductory book on sexuality that the Indian Church would do good to read. In addressing issues such as the authority of scripture in Christian living, the moral nature of sexual acts, the nexus between caste, masculinity, power and sexuality, and the course the Church must take to become a community that welcomes all, the book serves as a reminder of our place on this planet, calling for an ethically motivated self-reflective examination of oneself, drawing our attention back to who we are—sexual beings created by the divine.

The openly gay Episcopalian bishop Gene Robinson once said, "All of the biblical texts assumed everyone is heterosexual. Therefore to act in a same-sex manner is against one's nature, and there's something wrong with it."[1] This, to some degree, sums up the roots of the Church's attitude towards sexual orientation and gender diversity. Added to this is the fact that the Church has always had a love-hate relationship with sexuality in general.

Classical Roots of the Church's Teaching and Attitude

The early Church's dalliances with sexuality and gender diversity were undergirded by three major influences, namely, the Jewish, Roman and Greek. The words of Jesus as recorded in Christian Scriptures were probably the least important. Jesus himself said very little about sex. Moreover, his recorded words are somewhat contradictory. While asserting at times that marriage is ordained by God (Matthew 19:4–5), he specifically approves of those "who have made themselves eunuchs for the sake of the kingdom of heaven" (Matthew 19:12). He also characterises the unmarried as "equal to angels…and sons of the resurrection" (Luke 20:36).

The letters in the Pauline corpus carry far more weight than the Gospels if one were to identify the New Testament roots of Christian ideas and understanding about sex. Paul regarded sex as one of the earthly concerns that Christians should not give importance to. To him, the virgin life was best, but if people could not "exercise self-control, they should marry" (1 Corinthians 7:9). He condemned all extramarital sex, and categorically named adulterers and masturbators, along with thieves and drunkards, as people who were unworthy of heaven (cf. 1 Corinthians 6:9).

It was from mixing together the teachings of Jesus and Paul, Jewish writings, Greek and Roman philosophy, non-Christian mystery religions, and other religious traditions, that early converts developed their own ideas about sex. For instance, the Church father Tertullian was married but was careful to say that marriages were not prohibited to Christians. Yet, he regarded virginity as preferable. Marriage, to him, involved the "commixture of the flesh," and "consists of that which is the essence of fornication."

Hagiographical accounts from the period when the church underwent persecution describe women who cut their hair and dressed as men for much of their lives, and whose true sex was revealed only at death. St. Pelagia of Antioch, a repentant prostitute and a cross-dresser, was said to have lived for many years shut up and in solitude as Pelagius, a monk and a eunuch. This does not necessarily amount to giving legitimacy to cross-dressing or a bridging of the gender divide. In fact, it did not stop the Church from sexualising women martyrs. Preservation of their virginity and chastity at all costs was praised as the ultimate sacrifice.

Constantinian Shift in Sex

The most prominent Church Fathers gradually became strong proponents of asceticism. Jerome holds that by choosing virginity, a woman could move up the gender hierarchy, for "she will cease to be a woman and will be called man." John Chrysostom went on to argue that those who have sex with the same sex must be doing so because they are insane, and describes homosexuality as the worst of sins, greater than murder. Of course, we would have to look elsewhere if we were to accuse him of gender bias, as he asserts that women can be guilty of the 'sin' as much as men. Thus, "Chrysostom's learning and eloquence spans and sums up a long age of ever-growing moral outrage, fear and loathing of homosexuality."[2]

And then there was Augustine of Hippo.

Augustine considered women intellectually, morally, and even physically inferior. This led him to conclude that this difference in status was to be demonstrated in the only permissible position for intercourse, the woman underneath facing upwards and the man on top. Addressing his inability to control his own desires or give up his concubine, he also deduced that sexual desire is the one human craving that overcame both reason and will. And he continues to teach us even today that desire is the result of human sinfulness and disobedience to God, with God's grace the only possibility through which one can overcome it or any other human weakness.

Gender and Sexual Diversity (GSD) and the Medieval Church

Regressive and repressive attitudes held in the Church were made manifest in harsh and severe attitudes in Western and Eastern Christianity. This led to ambiguity with regard to celibacy as a prerequisite for the utmost dedication and commitment to God in priestly ministry. In Eastern Christianity, presbyters and deacons were allowed to marry before ordination, while bishops were chosen only from among celibate clergy. In Western Christianity, Leo the Great (c.400–461) wanted celibate clergy, but it was not enforced during his time. It was Pope Gregory VII (1073–85), who enforced it legally and effectively.

Clerical celibacy became the policy of the Western church from the twelfth century, with the campaign for clerical celibacy extended to homosexual relationships. The Third Lateran Council (1179) even decreed that clerics who could not give up homosexual activities were to surrender their clerical status, and laymen were to be excommunicated. Church and secular authorities increasingly defined homosexual actions as "crimes against nature."

Thomas Aquinas and the scholastics held that women had a stronger sex drive than men as well as a lesser capacity for reason. These made them, in Aquinas's words, "naturally subject to man." Women, though inferior, were also made by men, thereby making heterosexual love acceptable and 'natural.' Consequentially, this led to a strong emphasis on the divinely ordained and 'natural' inequality between men and women.

The Challenge Ahead

The above-mentioned historical trajectory of Christianity shows how the 'natural' and 'divinely-ordained' dichotomy prevalent in the Church's attitude towards sexual identity and gender diversity gradually became normative. Even momentous events that impact the Church's life, such as the Protestant Reformation or the Enlightenment or modern scientific know-how, could hardly make much of a dent.

We live in an increasingly intolerant world where differences are highlighted and then manipulated as a means for exclusion and control. There is a pressing need to understand the biblical, doctrinal and theological roots for the misogyny that hinders the Church's life and witness, and the homophobia and transphobia that makes many of our churches inaccessible for those who do fall outside of the binary mould that we try to fit them into. There is a need to understand the fluidity of gender identity and to acknowledge the creative and fulfilling potential that diversity can bring to the table. Only when it does that can the Church make a rightful claim to be inclusive and all-encompassing.

The book does not provide answers to difficult questions but, as Theodore claims, seeks to remove confusions and highlight patterns of interactions that lead to sexual injustice. Contesting such injustices is the challenge before us, before the Church.

Endnotes

* **John Lalnuntluanga** is a lay theologian of the Presbyterian Church of India, and works at the Gossner Theological College, Ranchi, Jharkhand teaching History and Missions. He also serves the ESHA-NCCI programme on Human Sexuality and Gender Identity as a core resource person.

[1] G. Jeffrey MacDonald, "Episcopal Bishop Champions Gay Marriage: PW Talks with Gene Robinson, *PW,* https://www.publishersweekly.com/pw/by-topic/authors/interviews/article/53696-episcopal-bishop-champions-gay-marriage-pw-talks-with-gene-robinson.html (accessed, 16 June 2020.)

[2] Robert H. Allen, *The Classical Origins of Modern Homophobia* (London: McFarland & Company, 2006), 187.

Bibliography

Althaus-Reid, Marcela. "'Let them talk!' Doing Liberation Theology from Latin American Closets." In *Liberation Theology and Sexuality*. Edited by Marcela Althaus-Reid. Hampshire: Ashgate Publishing Limited, 2006.

Ames, Lynda J. "Homo-Phobia, Homo-Ignorance, Homo-Hate: Heterosexism and AIDS." In *Preventing Heterosexism and Homophobia*. Edited by Esther D. Rothblum and Lynne A. Bond. London: SAGE Publications, 1996.

Armour, Ellen T. "Queer Bibles, Queer Scriptures? An Introductory Response." In *Bible Trouble. Queer Readings at the Boundaries of Biblical Scholarship*. Edited by Teresa J. Hornsby and Ken Stone. Atlanta: Society of Biblical Literature, 2011.

Anderson, Eric. *Inclusive Masculinity: The Changing Nature of Masculinities.* London: Routledge, 2009.

Anderson-Rajkumar, Evangeline. "Turning Bodies Inside Out: Contours of Womanist Theology." *Dalit Theology in the Twenty-first Century: Discordant Voices, Discerning Pathways*. Edited by Sathianathan Clarke, Deenabandhu Manchala, and Philip Vinod Peacock. New Delhi: Oxford University Press, 2010.

Apelqvist, Eva. *LGBTQ Families: The Ultimate Teen Guide.* Plymouth: Scarecrow Press, Inc., 2013.

Babu, Jeevan (Ed.). *Celebrating Family Life.* Delhi: ISPCK, 1994.

Baindur, Meera. "Homophobia and the Hindu Tradition: A Brief Discussion." In *Faiths Against Homophobia*. Edited by P. Mohan Larbeer, R. Christopher Rajkumar and The Aneka Team. BTESSC: Bangalore, 2015.

Balswick, Judith K. and Jack O. Balswick. *Authentic Human Sexuality: An Integrated Christian Approach*. Second edition. Illinois: InterVarsity Press, 2008.

Bergen, Jeremy M. *Ecclesial Repentance: The Churches Confront their Sinful Pasts*. New York: T&T Clark International, 2011.

Bohache, Thomas. *Christology from the Margins*. London: SCM Press, 2008.

Boopalan, Sundar John. *Memory, Grief and Agency: A Political Theological Account of Wrongs and Rites*. London: Palgrave Macmillan, 2017.

Bornstein, Kate. *Gender Outlaws*. New York: Routledge, 1994. Cited in Judith Butler, *Undoing Gender*. New York: Routledge, 2004.

Brock, Rita Nakashima. "Marriage Troubles." In *Body and Soul: Rethinking Sexuality in Justice-Love*. Edited by Marvin M. Ellison and Sylvia Thorson-Smith. Cleveland: The Pilgrim Press, 2003.

Browne, Kath and Catherine J. Nash (Eds.). *Queer Methods and Methodologies: Intersecting Queer Theories and Social Science* Research. London: Routledge, 2016.

Butler, Judith. *Gender Trouble: Feminism and the Subversion of Identity*. New York: Routledge, 2010.

Cahill, Lisa Sowle. *Between the Sexes: Foundations for a Christian Ethics of Sexuality*. New York: Paulist Press, 1985.

—————————. *Global Justice, Christology, and Christian* Ethics. New York: Cambridge University Press, 2013.

—————————. "Sexuality and Christian Ethics: How to Proceed." In *Sexuality and the Sacred: Sources for Theological Reflection*. Edited by James B. Nelson and Sandra P. Longfellow. Kentucky: Westminster/ John Knox Press, 1994.

Carr, David M. *The Erotic Word. Sexuality, Spirituality and the Bible*. New York: Oxford University Press, 2003.

Carson, D.A. *The Gospel According to John*. Michigan: William B. Eerdmans Publishing Company, 1991.

Carvalhaes, Claudio "Oh, Que Sera, Que Sera… A Limping A/Theological Thought in Brazil." In *Liberation Theology and Sexuality*. Edited by Marcela Althaus-Reid. Hampshire: Ashgate Publishing Limited, 2006.

Chakraborty, Chandrima. *Masculinity, Asceticism, Hinduism: Past and Present Imaginings of India*. Ranikhet: Permanent Black, 2011.

Chaudhary, Zahid. "Controlling the Ganymedes: The Colonial Gaze in J.R. Ackerley's Hindoo Holiday." In *Sexual Sites, Seminal Attitudes: Sexualities, Masculinities and Culture in South Asia*. Edited by Sanjay Srivastava. New Delhi: SAGE Publications, 2004.

Cheng, Patrick S. *An Introduction to Queer Theology: Radical Love*. New York: Seabury Books, 2011.

__________. *From Sin to Amazing Grace: Discovering the Queer Christ*. New York: Seabury Books, 2012.

__________. "The Rainbow Connection: Bridging Asian American and Queer Theologies." *Theology & Sexuality*. 17:3 (2011): 238-239.

Clarke, Sathianathan. "Dalits Overcoming Violation and Violence: A Contest between Overpowering and Empowering Identities in Changing India." *The Ecumenical Review*. 54:3 (2002): 278-295.

Coleman, Peter. *Christian Attitudes to Homo-sexuality*. London: SPCK, 1980.

Cooper, Davina. "Speaking Beyond Thinking: Citizenship, Governance and Lesbian and Gay Politics." In *Sexuality and the Law: Feminist Engagements*. Edited by Vanessa E. Munro and Carl F. Stychin. New York: Routledge-Cavendish, 2007.

Corvino, John. *What's Wrong with Homosexuality?* New York: Oxford University Press, 2013.

Culbertson, Philip. "Explaining Men." In *Sexuality and the Sacred: Sources for Theological Reflection*. Edited by James B. Nelson and Sandra P. Longfellow. Kentucky: Westminster/John Knox Press, 1994.

Das, Somen. *Christian Ethics and Indian Ethos*. New Delhi: ISPCK, 1994.

Dave, Naisargi N. *Queer Activism in India: A Story in the Anthropology of Ethics*. London: Duke University Press, 2012.

Dayam, Joseph Prabhakar. "Towards a Liberatory Christian Theology for Men: Interrogating the Gendered Self." In *Created in God's Image: From Hegemony to Partnership*. Edited by Patricia Sheerattan-Bisnauth and Philip Vinod Peacock. Geneva: WCC, 2010.

Dorapalli, David A. "Human Sexuality: Revisioning Queer Theologies in the Context of Homophobia." In *Disruptive Faith, Inclusive Communities: Church and Homophobia*. Edited by George Zachariah and Vincent Rajkumar. Bangalore/Delhi: CISRS/ISPCK, 2015.

Douglas, Kelly Brown. *Sexuality and the Black Church: A Womanist Perspective*. Maryknoll: Orbis Books, 2004.

Douglas, Mary. *Purity and Danger: An Analysis of the Concepts of Pollution and Taboo*. London/New York: Routledge and Kegan Paul, 1966. Cited in Peniel Rajkumar. *Dalit Theology and Dalit Liberation: Problems, Paradigms and Possibilities*. Surrey: Ashgate Publishing Limited, 2010.

Edwards, Tim. *Erotics and Politics: Gay Male Sexuality, Masculinity and Feminism*. NewYork: Taylor & Francis e-Library, 2004.

Ellens, J. Harold. *Sex in the Bible. A New Consideration*. London: Praeger, 2006.

Ellison, Marvin M. *Erotic Justice: A Liberation Ethic of Sexuality*. Kentucky: Westminster John Knox Press, 1996.

______________. *Making Love Just: Sexual Ethics for Perplexing Times*. Minneapolis: Fortress Press, 2012.

______________. "Practicing Safer Spirituality: Changing the Subject and Focusing on Justice." In *Out of the Shadows into the Light: Christianity and Homosexuality*. Edited by Miguel A. De La Torre. St. Louis: Chalice Press, 2009.

______________. *Same-Sex Marriage?: A Christian Ethical Analysis*. Cleveland: The Pilgrim Press, 2004.

______________. "What God Hath Joined: Notes on Same-Sex Marriage and Justice Making." In *Union Seminary Quarterly Review*. Volume 53. Numbers 3-4 (1999). Cited in George Zachariah, "Introduction," in *Disruptive Faith, Inclusive Communities: Church and Homophobia*. Edited by George Zachariah and Vincent Rajkumar. Bangalore/Delhi: CISRS/ISPCK, 2015.

______________ and Sylvia Thorson-Smith. "Wrestling to Dismantle Christian Homophobia and Heterosexism." In *Disruptive Faith, Inclusive Communities: Church and Homophobia*. Edited by George Zachariah and Vincent Rajkumar. Bangalore/Delhi: CISRS/ISPCK, 2015.

Eugene, Toinette. "While Love is Unfashionable: Ethical Implications of Black Spirituality and Sexuality." In *Sexuality and the Sacred: Sources for Theological Reflection*. Edited by James B. Nelson and Sandra P. Longfellow. Louisville: Westminster/John Knox Press, 1994.

Farley, Margaret A. *Just Love: A Framework for Christian Sexual Ethics*. New York: Continuum International Publishing Group, 2006.

Fineman, Martha A. *The Autonomy Myth: A Theory of Dependency*. New York: Free Press, 2003. Cited in Marvin M. Ellison, *Same-Sex Marriage?: A Christian Ethical Analysis*. Cleveland: The Pilgrim Press, 2004.

Flood, Gavin. *The Tantric Body: The Secret Tradition of Hindu Religion*. New York: I.B. Tauris & Co. Ltd., 2006.

Foucault, Michel. *Discipline and Punish: The Birth of the Prison*. Second edition. Translated by Alan Sheridan. New York: Vintage Books, 1995.

Fuchs, Eric. *Sexual Desire and Love: Origins and History of the Christian Ethic of Sexuality and Marriage*. Translated by Marsha Daigle. New York: The Seabury Press, 1983.

Ganguly, Debjani. *Caste, Colonialism and Counter-Modernity: Notes on a Postcolonial Hermeneutics of Caste*. London: Routledge, 2005.

Garton, Stephen. *Histories of Sexuality: Antiquity to Sexual Revolution*. London: Equinox Publishing Ltd, 2006.

Gasler, Chris. *Coming Out as Sacrament*. Kentucky: Westminster John Knox Press, 1998.

Gnanadason, Aruna. "Church and Sexual Morality." In *A Theological Reader on Human Sexuality and Gender Diversities: Envisioning Inclusivity*. Edited by Roger Gaikward and Thomas Ninan. Delhi/Nagpur: ISPCK/NCCI, 2017.

Gorringe, Tim "Liberation Ethics." *The Cambridge Companion to Christian Ethics*. Edited by Robin Gill. New York: Cambridge University Press, 2001.

Gorsline, Robin Hawley "1 and 2 Peter." In *The Queer Bible Commentary*. Edited by Deryn Guest, Robert E. Goss, Mona West and Thomas Bohache. London: SCM Press, 2006.

Goh, Joseph N. *Living Out Sexuality and Faith: Body Admissions of Malaysian Gay and Bisexual Men*. New York: Routledge, 2018.

Goss, Robert E. *Jesus Acted Up: A Gay and Lesbian Manifesto*. New York: HarperCollins Publishers, 1993.

_____________. *Queering Christ: Beyond Jesus Acted Up*. Cleveland: The Pilgrim Press, 2002.

_____________ and Deborah Krause. "The Pastoral Letters: 1 and 2 Timothy, and Titus." In *The Queer Bible Commentary*. Edited by Deryn Guest, Robert E. Goss, Mona West and Thomas Bohache. London: SCM Press, 2006.

Grosz, Elizabeth. "Bodies and Knowledges: Feminism and the Crisis of Reason." In *Feminist Epistemologies*. Edited by Linda Alcoff and Elizabeth Potter. New York: Routledge, 1993. Quoted in Esther Parajuli, *Sensuous Bodies and Sensuous Texts: Towards a Feminist Theological Understanding of Human Sexuality.* M.Th. Thesis: Senate of Serampore, 2014.

Grube, Dennis. *At the Margins of Victorian Britain: Politics, Immorality and Britishness in the Nineteenth Century.* London: I.B. Tauris & Co Ltd., 2013.

Guest, Deryn. *When Deborah Met Jael. Lesbian Biblical Hermeneutics.* London: SCM Press, 2005.

Harrison, Beverly Wildung. *Making the Connections: Essays in Feminist Social Ethics.* Edited by Carol S. Robb. Massachusetts: Beacon Press Books, 1985.

Havea, Jione. "Becoming Sensual with Public Study of Scriptures." In *Public and Sensual: Exploring Solutions. Bible Studies on Human Sexuality.* Edited by Christopher Rajkumar. Nagpur: NCCI, 2012.

Heyward, Carter. *Touching Our Strength: The Erotic as Power and the Love of God.* San Francisco: Harper & Row, 1989. Cited in Marvin M. Ellison, *Erotic Justice: A Liberation Ethic of Sexuality.* Kentucky: Westminster John Knox Press, 1996.

Ingram, Penelope. *The Signifying Body: Towards an Ethics of Sexual and Racial Difference.* New York: State of New York Press, 2008.

Irigaray, Luce. *An Ethic of Sexual Difference.* Translated by Carolyn Burke and Gillian C. Gill. New York: Cornell University Press, 1993.

Isherwood, Lisa and Elizabeth Stuart. *Introducing Body Theology.* Sheffield: Sheffield Academic Press, 1998.

Jain, Kajri. "Muscularity and its Ramifications: Mimetic Male Bodies in Indian Mass Culture." In *Sexual Sites, Seminal Attitudes: Sexualities, Masculinities and Culture in South Asia.* Edited by Sanjay Srivastava. New Delhi: SAGE Publications, 2004.

Jennings, Jr., Theodore W. *An Ethic of Queer Sex: Principles and Improvisations.* Illinois: Exploration Press, 2013.

__________________. *The Man Jesus Loved: Homoerotic Narratives from the New Testament.* Ohio: The Pilgrim Press, 2003.

__________________. "Reconstructing the Doctrine of Sin." In *The Other Side of Sin: Woundedness from the Perspective of the Sinned-Against.* Edited by Andrew Sung Park and Susan L. Nelson. Albany: State University of New York Press, 2001.

Jensen, David H. "The Bible and Sex." In *The Embrace of Eros. Bodies, Desires, and Sexuality in Christianity*. Edited by Margaret D. Kamitsuka. Minneapolis: Fortress Press, 2010.

Jeyaraj, Jesudason Baskar. "Biblical Concept, Imageries and Issues of Marriage." In *Marriage, Family and Church: Holistic Child Development*. Volume 2. Edited by Jesudason Baskar Jeyaraj. Delhi/Bangalore: ISPCK/CFCD, 2014.

Jordan, Mark D. *The Ethics of Sex*. Malden: Blackwell Publishing, 2002.

Joseph, Georvin. "Human Sexuality as a Garden of Celebrations." In *Public and Sensual: Exploring Solutions. Bible Studies on Human Sexuality*. Edited by Christopher Rajkumar. Nagpur: NCCI, 2012.

Kelly, Kevin T. *New Directions in Sexual Ethics: Moral Theology and the Challenge of AIDS*. London: Geoffrey Chapman, 1998.

Kimmel, Michael. "Masculinity as Homophobia: Fear, Shame, and Silence in the Construction of Gender Identity." In *Theorizing Masculinities*. Edited by Harry Brod and Michael Kaufman. London/Delhi: SAGE Publications, 1994.

______________. *The Gender of Desire. Essays on Male Sexuality*. Albany: State University of New York Press, 2005.

Koch, Timothy. "Cruising as Methodology: Homoeroticism and the Scriptures." In *The Queer Bible Commentary*. Edited by Deryn Guest, Robert E. Goss, Mona West and Thomas Bohache. London: SCM Press, 2006.

Kosnik, Anthony. Et al. *Human Sexuality: New Directions in American Catholic Thought*. New York: Paulist Press, 1977.

Kuttiyil, George Mathew. "Marriage as a Sacrament." In *Christian Family in Transition: Continuity and Discontinuity*. Faridabad: Dharma Jyoti Vidya Peeth, 2012.

L., Jayachitra "Dalit Theology as Anti-Caste Theology: Musings from Intersexual Dialogue in the Reign of God." In *Disruptive Faith, Inclusive Communities: Church and Homophobia*. Edited by George Zachariah and Vincent Rajkumar. Bangalore/Delhi: CISRS/ISPCK, 2015.

Lakeland, Paul. "'I Want to Be in That Number': Desire, Inclusivity and the Church." In *Proceedings of the Catholic Theological Society of America*. 66 (2011): 21-27. Cited in Sara Rosenau, "Queer Church: Failure and Becoming in the Body of Christ." In *Unlocking Orthodoxies for*

Inclusive Theologies. Edited by Robert E. Shore-Goss and Joseph N. Goh. London/New York: Routledge, 2020.

Lightsey, Pamela. *Our Lives Matter: A Womanist Queer Theology.* Wipf and Stock Publishers, 2015.

Loughlin, Gerard. "Introduction: End of Sex." In *Queer Theology: Rethinking the Western Body.* Edited by Gerard Loughlin. Victoria: Blackwell Publishing, 2007.

Maduro, Otto. "Once Again Liberating Theology? Towards a Latin American Liberation Theological Self-Criticism." In *Liberation Theology and Sexuality.* Edited by Marcela Althaus-Reid. Hampshire: Ashgate Publishing Limited, 2006.

Mallanaga, Vatsyayana. *Kamasutra.* Translated and edited by Wendy Doniger and Sudhir Kakar. New York: Oxford University Press, 2002. Cited in Margaret A. Farley, *Just Love: A Framework for Christian Sexual Ethics.* London: Continuum International Publishing Group, 2006.

May, Vivian M. *Pursuing Intersectionality, Unsettling Dominant Imaginaries.* New York: Routledge, 2015.

McCarthy, David Matzko. "The Relationship of Bodies: A Nuptial Hermeneutics of Same-sex Unions." In *Theology and Sexuality: Classic and Contemporary Readings.* Edited by Eugene F. Rogers, Jr. Massachusetts: Blackwell Publishers Ltd., 2002.

McMahon, Mercia "Trans Liberating Feminist and Queer Theologies." In *This is My Body: Hearing the Theology of Transgender Christians.* Edited by Christina Beardsley and Michelle O' Brien. London: Longman and Todd, 2016.

Melanchthon, Monica Jyotsna. "Sexuality." In *Created in God's Image: From Hegemony to Partnership.* Edited by Patricia Sheerattan-Bisnauth and Philip Vinod Peacock. Switzerland: WCC, 2010.

Menon, Nivedita "How Natural is Normal?" In *Because I Have a Voice: Queer Politics in India.* Edited by Arvind Narrain and Gautam Bhan. New Delhi: Yoda Press, 2005.

More, Megan. "The Transgendered Christ." In *Queering Christianity: Finding a Place at the Table for LGBTQI Christians.* Robert E. Shore-Goss, Thomas Bohache, Patrick S. Cheng, and Mona West. Oxford: Praeger, 2013.

Narrain, Arvind and Alok Gupta. "Introduction." In *Law Like Love: Queer Perspectives on Law.* Edited by Arvind Narrain and Alok Gupta. New Delhi: Yoda Press, 2011.

__________. "Queering Democracy." In *Law Like Love: Queer Perspectives on Law*. Edited by Arvind Narrain and Alok Gupta. New Delhi: Yoda Press, 2011.

Nelson, James B. *Body Theology*. Kentucky: Westminster/John Knox Press, 1992.

__________. *Embodiment: An Approach to Sexuality and Christian Theology*. Minneapolis: Augsburg Publishing House, 1978.

__________. *The Intimate Connection: Male Sexuality, Masculine Spirituality*. London: SPCK, 1992).

O'Connor. D. J. *Aquinas and Natural Law*. London: Macmillan & Co Ltd., 1967.

Parker, Rebecca. "Making Love as a Means of Grace: Women's Reflections." In *Sexuality: A Reader*. Edited by Karen Lebacqz. Ohio: The Pilgrim Press, 1999.

Perkins, Benjamin. "Coming Out, Lazarus's and Ours: Queer Reflections of a Psychospiritual Political Journey." In *Take Back the Word: A Queer reading of the Bible*. Edited by Robert E. Goss and Mona West. Ohio: The Pilgrim Press, 2000.

Pharr, Suzanne. *Homophobia: A Weapon of Sexism*. California: Chardon Press, 1997.

Pires, Frederico Pieper "Liberation Theology, Modernity and Sexual Difference." In *Liberation Theology and Sexuality*. Edited by Marcela Althaus-Reid. Hampshire: Ashgate Publishing Limited, 2006.

Presbyterian Church of Aotearoa New Zealand. *Sexual Ethics*. Wellington: Presbyterian Church of Aotearoa New Zealand.

Rajkumar, Peniel. *Dalit Theology and Dalit Liberation: Problems, Paradigms and Possibilities*. Surrey: Ashgate Publishing Limited, 2010.

Rajkumar, R. Christopher. "Indian Ecumenical Response to Human Sexuality." In *Disruptive Faith, Inclusive Communities: Church and Homophobia*. Edited by George Zachariah and Vincent Rajkumar. Bangalore/Delhi: CISRS/ISPCK, 2015.

Ratzinger, Joseph. "The Transmission of Divine Revelation." In *Commentary on the Documents of Vatican II*. Volume 3. Edited by Herbert Vorgrimler. New York: Herder & Herder, 1969. Cited in Margaret A. Farley, *Just Love: A Framework for Christian Sexual Ethics*. New York: Continuum International Publishing Group, 2006.

Reay, Lewis. "Towards a Transgender Theology: Que(e)rying the Eunuchs." In *Trans/Formations*. Edited by Marcella Althaus-Reid and Lisa Isherwood. London: SCM Press, 2009.

Revathy. *A Life in Transactivism*. New Delhi: Zubaan, 2016.

Ribas, Mario. "Liberating Mary, Liberating the Poor." In *Liberation Theology and Sexuality*. Edited by Marcela Althaus-Reid. Hampshire: Ashgate Publishing Limited, 2006.

Ricoeur, Paul. *Symbolism of Evil*. Translated by Emerson Buchanan. New York: Harper & Row, 1967. Cited in Margaret A. Farley, *Just Love: A Framework for Christian Sexual Ethics*. London: Continuum International Publishing Group, 2006.

Rogers, Jr. Eugene F., *Sexuality and the Christian Body: Their Way into the Triune God*. Massachusetts: Blackwell Publishers Ltd., 1999.

Rubin, Gayle. "Thinking Sex: Notes for a Radical Theory of the Politics of Sexuality." In *Pleasure and Danger: Exploring Female Sexuality*. Edited by Carole S. Vance. Boston: Routledge & K. Paul, 1984. Cited in Theodore W. Jennings, Jr., *An Ethic of Queer Sex: Principles and Improvisations*. Illinois: Exploration Press, 2013.

Ruether, Rosemary Radford "Homophobia, Heterosexism, and Pastoral Practice." In *Sexuality and the Sacred. Sources for Theological Reflection*. Edited by James B. Nelson and Sandra P. Longfellow. Kentucky: John Knox Press, 1994.

Russell, Letty M. *The Future of Partnership*. Philadelphia: The Westminster Press, 1979.

Samuel, Joshua. "Towards a Queer Dalit Theology: Dialogue and Solidarity Among the Margins." In *Bangalore Theological Forum*. Volume LI. Number 2 (2019): 142-167.

Samuel, Joshua. *Untouchable Bodies, Resistance, and Liberation: A Comparative Theology of Divine Possessions*. (Boston: Brill, 2020).

Shankar, Gopi. "Definitions—Understanding Gender, Sex and Sexuality." *A Theological Reader on Human Sexuality and Gender Diversities: Envisioning Inclusivity*. Edited by Roger Gaikward and Thomas Ninan. Delhi/Nagpur: ISPCK/NCCI, 2017.

Sharma, Arvind. "Homosexuality and Hinduism." In *Homosexuality and Word Religions*. Edited by Arlene Swidler. Pennsylvania: Trinity Press International, 1993.

Shore-Goss, Robert E, Thomas Bohache, Patrick S. Cheng, and Mona West (Eds.). *Queering Christianity: Finding a Place at the Table for LGBTQI Christians.* Oxford: Praeger, 2013.

Sichtermann, Barbara, "Rape and Sexuality." In *The Polity Reader in Gender Studies.* Cambridge: Polity Press, 2002.

Singh, Manu and Shilpi Singh. "Faith and Sexuality: Perspectives from Hinduism." In *Faiths Against Homophobia.* Edited by P. Mohan Larbeer, R. Christopher Rajkumar and The Aneka Team. BTESSC: Bangalore, 2015.

Spencer, Dan "Church at the Margins." In *Sexuality and the Sacred: Sources for Theological Reflection.* Edited by James B. Nelson and Sandra P. Longfellow. Kentucky: Westminster/John Knox Press, 1994.

Spencer, Daniel T. "A Gay Male Ethicist's Response to Queer Readings of the Bible." In *The Queer Bible Commentary.* Edited by Deryn Guest, Robert E. Goss, Mona West and Thomas Bohache. London: SCM Press, 2006.

Srivastava, Sanjay (Ed.). "Non-Gandhian Sexuality, Commodity Cultures and a 'Happy Married Life': Masculine and Sexual Cultures in the Metropolis." In *Sexual Sites, Seminal Attitudes: Sexualities, Masculinities and Culture in South Asia.* New Delhi: SAGE Publications, 2004.

Stone, Ken. "What the Homosexuality Debates Really Say about the Bible." In *Out of the Shadows into the Light: Christianity and Homosexuality.* Edited by Miguel A. De La Torre. St. Louis: Chalice Press, 2009.

__________. "Queer Commentary and Biblical Interpretation: An Introduction." In *Queer Commentary and the Hebrew Bible.* Edited by Ken Stone. Ohio: The Pilgrim Press, 2001.

Stuart, Elizabeth and Adrian Thatcher. *People of Passion: What the Churches teach about Sex.* London: Mowbray, 1997.

__________. "Sacramental Flesh." In *Queer Theology: Rethinking the Western Body.* Edited by Gerard Loughlin. Victoria: Blackwell Publishing Ltd., 2007.

__________. "The Priest at the Altar: Eucharistic Erasure of Sex." In *Trans/formations.* Edited by Lisa Isherwood and Marcella Althaus-Reid. London: SCM Press, 2009.

Susannah Cornwall, "Apophasis and Ambiguity: The Unknowingness of Transgender." In *Trans/Formations.* Edited by Marcella Althaus-Reid and Lisa Isherwood. London: SCM Press, 2009.

Thatcher, Adrian. *Liberating Sex: A Christian Sexual Theology*. London: SPCK, 1993.

Thorson-Smith, Sylvia. "Becoming 'Possessed: Toward Sexual Health and Well-Being'" In *Body and Soul: Rethinking Sexuality as Justice-Love*. Edited by Marvin M. Ellison and Sylvia Thorson-Smith. Oregon: Wipf & Stock, 2003.

Torre, Miguel A. De La. *A Lily among the Thorns: Imagining a New Christian Sexuality*. San Francisco: Jossey-Bass, 2007.

__________. *Doing Christian Ethics from the Margins*. New York: Orbis Books, 2014.

__________. *Latina/o Social Ethics: Moving Beyond Eurocentric Moral Thinking*. Texas: Baylor University Press, 2010.

__________. *Liberating Sexuality: Justice Between the Sheets*. Saint Louis: Chalice Press, 2016.

__________. *Reading the Bible from the Margins*. New York: Orbis Books, 2003.

Vanita, Ruth. "Introduction: Ancient Indian Materials." In *Same-Sex Love in India: A Literary History*. Edited by Ruth Vanita and Saleem Kidwai. Haryana: Penguin Random House India Pvt. Ltd., 2008.

__________. "Vatsyayana's *Kamasutra*." In *Same-Sex Love in India: A Literary History*. Edited by Ruth Vanita and Saleem Kidwai. Haryana: Penguin Random House India Pvt. Ltd., 2008.

__________. "Vishnu Sharma's *Panchatantra* (Sanskrit)." In *Same-Sex Love in India: A Literary History*. Edited by Ruth Vanita and Saleem Kidwai. Haryana: Penguin Random House India Pvt. Ltd., 2008.

Varghese, Winnie. *A Journey of Faith: Church and* Homosexuality. Bangalore: BTESSC, 2014.

__________. "Eliminating Homophobia in the Indian Church: The Goodness of the Body." In *Disruptive Faith, Inclusive Communities: Church and Homophobia*. Edited by George Zachariah and Vincent Rajkumar. Bangalore/Delhi: CISRS/ISPCK, 2015.

Varughese, Shiju Sam. "The Queerness of Creation: Science, Religion and Human Sexuality." In *Disruptive Faith, Inclusive Communities: Church and Homophobia*. Edited by George Zachariah and Vincent Rajkumar. Bangalore/Delhi: CISRS/ISPCK, 2015.

Vuola, Elina. *Limits of Liberation: Feminist Theology and the Ethics of Poverty and* Reproduction. London: Sheffield Academic Press, 2002.

__________. "Thinking *Otherwise*: Dussel, Liberation Theology, and Feminism." In *Thinking from the Underside of History. Enrique Dussel's Philosophy of Liberation.* Edited by Linda Martín Alcoff and Eduardo Mendieta. New York: Rowman & Littlefield Publishers, Inc., 2000.

Ward, Graham. "Bodies: The Displaced Body of Jesus Christ." In *Radical Orthodoxy: A New Theology.* Edited by John Milbank, Catherine Pickstock and Graham Ward. New York: Taylor & Francis e-Library, 2002.

__________. "There Is No Sexual Difference." In *Queer Theology: Rethinking the Western Body.* Edited by Gerard Loughlin. Victoria: Blackwell Publishing Ltd., 2007.

Weinberg, George. *Society and the Healthy Homosexual.* New York: St. Martin's Press, 1972.

West, Mona. "Reading the Bible as a Queer American: Social Location in Hebrew Scriptures." In *Theology and Sexuality* 10 (March 1999). Cited in George Zachariah, "Introduction," in *Disruptive Faith, Inclusive Communities: Church and Homophobia.* Edited by George Zachariah and Vincent Rajkumar. Bangalore/Delhi: CISRS/ISPCK, 2015.

__________. "Shaped by the Word." In *Out of the Shadows into the Light: Christianity and Homosexuality.* Edited by Miguel A. De La Torre. St. Louis: Chalice Press, 2009.

Williams, Monnica. "Homosexuality Anxiety: A Misunderstood Form of OCD." In *Leading-Edge Health Education Issues.* Edited by Lennard V. Sebeki. New York: Nova Science Publishers, Inc., 2008.

Williams, Robert. *Just as I Am: A Practical Guide to being Out, Proud and Christian.* New York: Harper Perennial, 1992. Cited in Patrick S. Cheng, *From Sin to Amazing Grace: Discovering the Queer Christ.* New York: Seabury Books, 2012.

Wuest, Kenneth. *Wuest's Word Studies in the Greek New Testament.* Volume III. Michigan: William. B. Eerdmans Publishing Co., 1975.

Zachariah, George "Introduction." In *Disruptive Faith, Inclusive Communities: Church and Homophobia.* Edited by George Zachariah and Vincent Rajkumar. Bangalore/Delhi: CISRS/ISPCK, 2015.

Unpublished Sources

Parajuli, Esther. *Sensuous Bodies and Sensuous Texts: Towards a Feminist Theological Understanding of Human Sexuality*. M.Th. Thesis: Senate of Serampore, 2014.

Jongte, Rochhuathanga. *Imagining Redemptive Masculinity: Towards a Tribal Theological Anthropology*. M.Th. Thesis: Senate of Serampore, 2014.

Interviews

Divya. Interviewed by the author. Bangalore. March 4, 2017.

Romal Laisram. Interviewed by the author. Bangalore. March 9, 2017.

Electronic Resources

Anderson, Dianna E. "I'm Not Your Ally: The Problem of Ally-As-Identity. http://diannaeanderson.net/blog/2013/10/im-not-your-ally-the-problem-of-ally-as-identity

Benjamin, Rahul. "Church to oppose legalization of gay sex in India." In *Christian Today*. http://www.christiantoday.co.in/article/church.to.oppose.legalization.of.gay.sex.in.india/4118.htm

Bijay Kumar Minj, "India Church unhappy with legalization of homosexuality," *UCA News,* https://www.ucanews.com/news/india-church-unhappy-with-legalization-of-homosexuality/83280

Clarke, Sathianathan. "Viewing the Bible Through the Eyes and Ears of Subalterns in India." *Biblical Interpretation*. 10:3 (2002): 259.https://brill.com/abstract/journals/bi/10/3/article-p245_2.xml

Galbin, Alexandra. "An Introduction to Social Constructionism." In *Social Research Reports*. Volume 26 (December 2014). https://www.researchgate.net/publication/283547838_AN_INTRODUCTION_TO_SOCIAL_CONSTRUCTIONISM.

Hackenberg, Amy J. and Brian R. Lawler. "An Ethics of Liberation emerging from a Radical Constructivist Foundation," 4. https://www.academia.edu/11978864/An_ethics_of_liberation_emerging_from_a_radical_constructivist_foundation_2002_

Harris, Mary "LGBT Community Pens Open Letter to the Orthodox Church." *Greek Greece Reporter,* http://greece.greekreporter.com/2016/06/24/lgbt-community-pens-open-letter-to-the-greek-orthodox-church/

Herek, Gregory M. "Beyond "Homophobia": Thinking about Sexual Prejudice and Stigma in the Twenty-First Century." In *Journal of NSRC: Sexuality Research & Social Policy*. Volume 1. Issue 2 (April, 2004). http://facultysites.dss.ucdavis.edu/~gmherek/rainbow/html/Herek_2004_SRSP.pdf.

"History of Gender Minorities in India – Gopi Shankar M," *Center for Indic Studies*, September 15, 2018, video, 7:20, https://www.youtube.com/watch?v=c7lYSwEaXzA&t=1188s

Iyer, Bhagirath "At 12 She Wanted to Die. Today She is Inspiring Hundreds to Fight for Transgender Rights & Justice." *The Better India*, https://www.thebetterindia.com/21961/how-jagadeesh-became-akkai-padmashali-and-a-transgender-activist-was-born/

McElwee, Joshua J. "Gutierrez at Vatican: Church must be Samaritan, reaching out to others." *National Catholic Reporter*. https://www.ncronline.org/blogs/ncr-today/gutierrez-vatican-church-must-be-samaritan-reaching-out-others

Mehra, Sunil, Manu Joseph, and Saira Menezes. "What's Burning?" *Outlook India Magazine*. http://www.outlookindia.com/article. aspx?206676

Paul, Samuel Ragland. "God in Dirty Places: Inter-Caste Marriage." *God in Dirty Places,* https://gindp.blogspot.com/2020/06/day-25-god-in-dirty-places-inter-caste.html

Purkayastha, Shramana Das. ""Against the Order of Nature"?: Postcolonial State, Section 377 and the Homosexual Subject." In *Rupkatha Journal.* Volume VI. No. 1 (2014). http://rupkatha.com/V6/n1/12_Section_377_Homosexuality.pdf

"Pope Francis says Christians 'must apologize' to gay people." *DW.* https://www.dw.com/en/pope-francis-says-christians-must-apologize-to-gay-people/a-19358739

Rawade, Priscilla. "God in Dirty Places: Filthy Love and a Wrestling God." *God in Dirty Places,* https://gindp.blogspot.com/2020/06/day-24-god-in-dirty-places-filthy-love.html

Roen, Nick. "Homophobia Has No Place in the Church." *Desiring God.* https://www.desiringgod.org/articles/homophobia-has-no-place-in-the-church

Sharma, Rohit "The Public and Constitutional Conundrum: A Case-note on the *Naz Foundation* Judgment." In *NUJS Law Review.* 2 NUJS L. Rev.

445 (July-September 2009). http://www.commonlii.org/in/journals/NUJSLawRw/2009/25.pdf

Tellis, Ashley. "Disrupting the Dinner Table: Re-thinking the 'Queer Movement' in Contemporary India." In *Jindal Global Law Review*. Volume 4. Issue 1 (August 2012). http://www.academia.edu/4066880/Disrupting_the_Dinner_Table_Rethinking_the_Queer_Movement_in_Contemporary_India

————————————. "The bad sex award goes to gay Indian men." *DNA* https://www.dnaindia.com/lifestyle/report-the-bad-sex-award-goes-to-gay-indian-men-1749720

————————————. "The politics of cinematic visibility." *DNA* http://www.dnaindia.com/lifestyle/report-the-politics-of-cinematic-visibility-1676028

————————————. "Should even we live happily ever after?" *DNA*, https://www.dnaindia.com/analysis/column-should-even-we-live-happily-ever-after-1688029

Wendt, Fritz. "The Politics of a New 'Family Values'—Matthew 10:24-39." *Political Theology Network*. https://politicaltheology.com/the-politics-of-a-new-family-values-matthew-1024-39-fritz-wendt/

"Who's Afraid of Ashley Tellis," *Lavidabibhishikha*. https://lavidabibhishikha.wordpress.com/2012/10/12/whos-afraid-of-ashley-tellis/

Wong, Curtis M. "The History and Meaning of The Rainbow Pride Flag." *Huffpost. https://www.huffpost.com/entry/rainbow-pride-flag-history_n_5b193aafe4b0599bc6e124a0*

Zachariah, George. "Church: A Rainbow Community of the Beloved and Equals." https://www.academia.edu/2644190/Church_A_Rainbow_Community_of_the_Beloved_and_Equals